revive
YOUR GARDEN

DEDICATION

·······································

*For Katy,
Freddie and Harry*

revive
YOUR GARDEN

How to bring your outdoor space back to life

NICK BAILEY

Photography by Jonathan Buckley

KYLE BOOKS

First published in Great Britain in 2018
by Kyle Cathie Limited
Part of Octopus Publishing Group Limited
Carmelite House, 50 Victoria Embankment
London EC4Y 0DZ
www.kylebooks.co.uk

10 9 8 7 6 5 4 3 2 1

ISBN 978 0 85783 432 4

Editor: Judith Hannam
Editorial Assistant: Isabel Gonzalez-Prendergast
Copy Editor: Clare Churly
Designer: Jenny Semple
Photographer: Jonathan Buckley
Illustrator: Alyson Hamilton
Production: Nic Jones and Gemma John

A Cataloguing in Publication record for this title is available from the British Library.

Colour reproduction by ALTA London
Printed and bound in China by 1010 International Printing Ltd.

contents

introduction

The perpetual evolution of gardens is perhaps their most seductive and beguiling virtue. They change every day. And those subtle cumulative shifts are what feeds into and enriches their unique sense of place. Gardens become their own entities both giving to and taking from the wider environment in which they reside. Complex relationships develop between plants, places and those that attend them. But, left unmanaged, a new and natural evolution takes hold as Mother Nature sets to work re-wilding what was once meticulously ordered. Weeds emerge, tree seedlings take root, brambles encroach and shrubs become overblown and ragged as they battle with native invaders. Left too long and Mother Nature will have her way, returning the garden to forest, but catch the plot, bed or border in time and it can be revived.

I've spent nearly 30 years holding gardens back from the brink of wildness and revitalising those that have tipped over the edge. It's not always easy but breathing life back into an ailing plot couldn't be more rewarding. Rather than start from scratch there is something utterly fulfilling about regenerating what is there, thus holding onto the spirit of the place. Giving plants, soils and structures that have battled it out alone a helping hand feels good and for every bit of effort we put in, the garden and its plants will pay us back tenfold.

A garden revival may appear overwhelming at first but it can be broached in manageable stages (see page 214). Before starting any work it's worth taking some time to understand the garden, its foibles and what it holds. There is no perfect moment to begin but the longer you leave it the more you'll understand the site. I'm not promoting procrastination here but rather observation. Rushing ahead at a particular time of year such as late winter may lead to damaging or destroying plants such as spring or autumn bulbs which are yet to emerge. Equally, once late winter has passed the opportunity to move or prune many shrubs has ceased. So the decision comes down to how long you are prepared to wait and how significant the garden's existing plant stock is to you. Another key consideration is which elements of the work you are going to carry out yourself. Budget or inclination may determine that you get your hands dirty and do the bulk yourself but certain jobs such as large scale tree pruning or major hard landscaping are best left to the professionals. That said, the lion's share of what I'm recommending can be carried out with limited experience and a virtually zero budget.

I want to share my experiences and guide you through reviving your own piece of the world, step by step. No matter whether you've gardened your whole life or you are new to it, I hope to present you with fresh ideas and approaches that will see your garden revived.

The Revival Process

1. Analyse what's worth keeping, improving or removing.

2. Clear debris and check plants for health and vigour.

3. Prune, move or remove existing plants.

4. Eradicate annual, perennial, woody and climbing weeds.

5. Consider how to 'layer in' new plants to the space.

6. Analyse and improve the soil ready for planting.

7. Plants pruned earlier in the season put on fresh growth.

8. With new planting the area is fully revived!

Understand legal restrictions, page 16

Understand your plants, page 18

Understand your microclimates, page 14

Identify key plants, page 32

Understand your soil, page 29

understand

No matter whether you've taken on a new garden or you're looking to upgrade what you already have, the process of Revival is the same. It starts by understanding the various elements of the garden. This process encompasses all aspects of an existing plot as indicated by the circled areas to the left. Getting to know your green-space is a surprisingly rewarding process and will set you on course to getting the very best out of your garden. So, what are you waiting for? Let's bring your garden back to life!

Identify weeds, page 18

Beginning Your Garden Revival

Bringing a tired and forgotten garden back to life is an exciting and rewarding journey. It's more than simply a makeover. It is a complex but achievable process that takes the best of what is already there, improves it and adds more, resulting in a garden that is rich in spirit, soul, legacy and life. With the promise of all this ahead it's tempting to launch straight into the dramatic, instant stuff, such as redesigns and radical prunes, but take a moment before you begin. To get the most out of the garden in the future it's worth taking the time to fully understand all of its foibles, now. By understanding it you can make the most of all it has to offer while designing your way round its limitations. Considering the following questions and many more, will help you to do that:

● Which bit of the garden gets the most sun?

● How do the views out of the garden change when the leaves fall?

● Will the soil support acid-loving plants?

● Is the shed in the most practical place?

● Are these plants pretty self-seeders or pernicious weeds?

● Why are plants in that corner looking so sick?

● Which of the existing plants are worth keeping?

● Which of the shrubs can be pruned back into life?

● Should that paving be replaced, improved or removed?

Going through the process of 'understanding' the plot with these and numerous other questions will put you on track to create a garden that works for you.

Overgrown and neglected areas may contain untold treasures so it's wise to give the plot time to reveal itself before launching into a revival.

Location and microclimate

Every garden I've ever owned, managed or loved has had its own unique set of oddities – the shady wet corner, the bit that's overlooked by the neighbours, or the ailing but legally protected tree that your local authority won't let you remove. Understanding these aspects is the first step towards reviving a garden, but don't forget to consider the wider environment the plot is set in, too. A garden in a Northern European city centre will have very different temperatures and rainfall than a plot set just 10 miles outside the city limits. If you are new to the area, neighbours can give you a sense of the long-term weather patterns, but a quick online search is useful, too. All of these factors, both macro and micro, will give you a sense of the opportunities and restrictions inherent to the garden.

Orientation and light are the first aspects of your plot to consider in detail. The rising sun will, of course, tell you where east is. The rest you can figure out from there. If possible, keep an eye on the track of the sun over a few months to truly understand when and where the garden is well lit. My own garden faces north-east, which may seem like a curse but it gets full sun for nearly five hours in the morning until it falls into shade around 2 p.m. when the sun is higher than the house and strikes the back half of the garden for the remainder of the day. This pattern occurs through the summer months, but winter is a different story. For three months the sun barely rises high enough to hit the garden. There is reflected light, and plenty of it, but no direct sun. These differing 'sun tracks' have determined how I've designed and planted the garden and observations of your plot will arm you with the information you need to make your own planting decisions. It will also help to determine the best position for new elements, such as seating areas, a glasshouse or a pond.

A rough scale sketch of the garden noting when and where the sun appears will highlight the limitations and opportunities you have before you. It is also worth noting which plants are surviving and thriving, and where. A batch of lush happy ferns is likely to indicate dappled to full shade, whereas a mass of self-seeded opium poppies is more likely to occur in full sun. Let the plants as well as the sun guide you as to the levels of light on your plot.

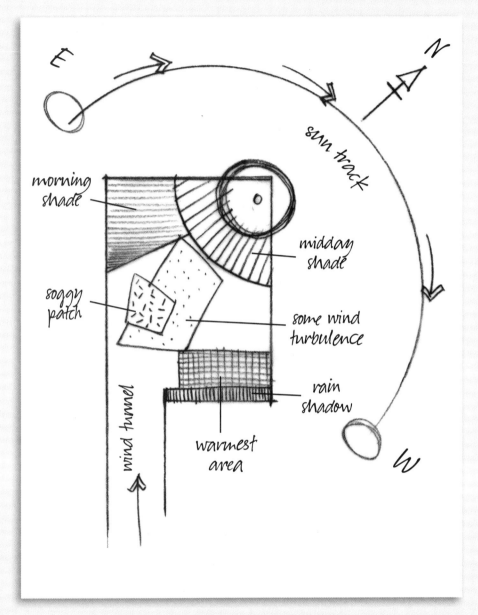

As important as the 'sun track' are the microclimates within the garden. These are simply areas with their own unique sets of light, precipitation and wind. It is worth noting these on your sketch, too. Again, plants and your own observations will help you identify each of these areas. Hot and dry microclimates, unsurprisingly, tend to be generated in protected, walled south-facing areas, whereas cool, shadier climes can be found against north-facing walls with water nearby.

Sun is far from the only factor determining microclimates, though. Wind is a significant element, too. Have a wander around on windy days and see where the 'wind tunnels' are in the garden. These are more often than not narrow spaces that channel the wind and increase its vigour. And if the garden is walled or fenced (as most are in Europe) then there are likely to be areas of turbulence caused by wind leapfrogging over the barrier and violently swirling around for some 5m on the other side of it.

Levels of precipitation are also vital. You may be living in a high-rainfall area but the fixed elements of your plot, such as buildings and trees, will affect how much water actually falls direct into the garden. High walls cause 'rain shadow', a difficult microclimate to overcome. It is essentially an area of soil at the base of a wall that never receives even the tiniest drop of rain. Compound this with the heat coming out of the wall and you have a difficult, but not unresolvable, horticultural challenge on your hands.

Other microclimates to look out for and note on your sketch plan include: east- and west-facing walls that are bathed in light or receive none at all for equal parts of the day and the understorey of trees, which is usually dry and shady. Also notable are damp and shady areas, hot and dry bits and highly protected spaces. There are suggested plants for all these difficult microclimates in the Refresh chapter (pages 160–87) so do not despair, there is a plant adapted or adaptable to nearly every situation.

Large-scale tree pruning work is usually best left to expert arboriculturalists.

LIMITATIONS

In addition to understanding the opportunities and limitations of your garden in terms of its plants, soil and microclimate, there is another significant series of factors to consider. These are the dull but unavoidable elements, such as services and your legal rights. Unappealing as this stuff is, it is much better to address it from the outset rather than discovering a restricting factor midway through your garden revival.

The first things to consider are the services either feeding or passing through the property. These could include electric cables (sub-surface and overhead), telephone cables (sub-surface and overhead), water pipes, data cables, irrigation systems, gas pipes, waste pipes and soakaways. If you are really lucky there might be a 'services' plan of the property. If not, it is worth contacting both the service providers and your local authority to understand the routes of pipes and cables into and out of your property. Failing this, try carrying out small delicate excavations close to the house where the pipes and cables emerge to get an initial sense of in which direction they are heading. Small, carefully excarated trenches may then

reveal the whereabouts of the underground services. If none of this works – which has happened to me on garden-build projects – consider calling in a water diviner. I cannot begin to explain how or why this works, but in my experience it does. There are also specialist firms who through means of powerful detection equipment can identify pipes and cables. This process of identification is, frankly, dull, but if you damage a service pipe or cable on your property you are liable and the repair costs can run to thousands – money that could be better spent on plants!

Next on the list of boring but necessary tasks is to establish whether there are any legal restrictions relating to your property. The two you are most likely to encounter in the UK are rights of way and Tree Preservations Orders.

Your deeds and other documents relating to the property should highlight any rights of way but failing this your local authority will have the information. If you do have an existing right of way that is going to compromise what you are hoping to do in the garden, it is sometimes possible to 'buy out' the right of way from its owner, which may be a neighbour, landowner or the local authority.

Tree Preservation Orders (TPOs) are a more straightforward matter. Contact the Tree Preservation Officer at your local authority and they will be able to let you know if you have TPOs applying to trees on your property. TPOs are usually put in place to protect large or older trees but can apply to any tree. They prevent any work being carried out (including the tiniest pruning job) without consent from the council. They also prevent the soil level under a protected tree being raised or excavated by more than 250mm. TPOs, rightly, are taken very seriously and infringement can incur a hefty fine, so it is worth checking!

The local authority will also be able to tell you if your property falls within a conservation area, in which case it is likely all the trees on your property will be protected. This is, however, not insurmountable as works to a 'conservation tree' are more likely to be granted than works to a TPO tree.

PLANNING PERMISSION

If you are planning on installing any structures then it is a good idea to set this in motion with your local authority early on. In the UK planning permission in the garden can be a tricky subject. In most instances you are allowed to install impermanent structures (fences, pergolas, sheds) that are under 2m tall without having to get planning consent. However, it is always worth checking to avoid having to pull down your masterpiece.

The other unavoidable potential limitation is the impact of the properties that surround you. Their windows, trees and hedges can have a profound impact on your garden so it is worth an initial assessment. 'Right-to-light' disputes in relation to tall trees or hedges are common but now thankfully dealt with direct by the local authority, as long as you can prove you've attempted to address the situation (peacefully) yourself.

NEIGHBOURS

Any tree, shrub or climber that is overhanging your garden from a neighbour's can be removed (level with the boundary). The legal restriction here is that you must return the prunings to your neighbour. Although this makes legal sense, as the prunings are their property, it does not, from experience, go down well to just dump the lot over the fence – do let your neighbours know what you are up to!

It is a worthwhile exercise to wander the plot to see which bits of the garden are overlooked and which are private. This

process can then inform later design decisions to block certain views or make more of others. It goes without saying, but do bear in mind that views in and out of the garden will change dramatically depending on season, leaf fall and the amount of evergreens surrounding the plot.

Avoid neighbourly clashes by discussing pruning and contruction work before it starts.

Weed or worthwhile plant?

One of the most common challenges when starting a garden revival is distinguishing between the weeds and the worthwhile plants. All too often the temptation is to go for a complete bed and border clearance, which may remove the weeds, but it also destroys untold horticultural wonders. Then there is the age-old dilemma of what is a weed and what is a plant? This question is akin to the adage 'one person's rubbish is another's treasure'. Certain species that I've allowed to romp away in the gardens that I've managed have been promptly removed by the new head gardener – it's nearly all down to taste, though there are some nasties that even the most quirky gardener would struggle to convince anyone were worthwhile plants.

One of the challenges in picking the wannabes from the wonders in a bunch of germinating seedlings is that the good and the bad can look quite similar. The seedling images (opposite) go some way to help identify a few of the most common weeds and useful self-seeders you are likely to discover on your plot. Armed with this understanding you can then make your call on which are 'your plants' and 'your weeds' and make the appropriate removals. See page 92 for dealing with and eradicating different types of weeds.

It is also worth noting that hand removal is not always a good idea if you have a lot of useful and useless plants growing cheek by jowl. Tugging out a seedling of a dead nettle next to a lovely forget-me-not can disrupt the roots of the forget-me-not to the extent that it is also killed off. Better in these instances to get in with a pair of snips and chop the weed at the base to kill it off. Perennial weeds may re-shoot but can then be carefully treated with a weed wipe. See page 94 for a range of weed management techniques.

WORTHWHILE PLANT

1. Viola
2. Geranium
3. Snowdrop
4. Pulmonaria
5. Aqualegia
6. Crocus
7. Helleborus

WEED

8. Dock
9. Alliaria Petiolata
10. Clevers
11. Sow Thistle

WORTHWHILE PLANT

1. Lily of the Valley
2. Ivy
3. Poppy (Papaver somniferum)
4. Carex pendula

WEED

5. Epilobium
6. Groundsel
7. Geranium robertianum
8. Bittercress
9. Ash (Fraxinus)

WORTHWHILE PLANT

1. Arum italicum
2. Forget-me-not
3. Lathyrus
4. Tellina grandiflora
5. Helleborus

WEED

6. Alliaria petiolata (mustard garlic)
7. Geum
8. Bramble
9. Acer pseudoplatanus
10. Dock

WORTHWHILE
PLANT
....
1. Allium triquetrum

WEED
....
2. Dead Nettle
3. Bittercress
4. Groundsel
5. Chickweed
6. Euphorbia peplus
7. Cerastium

Identify and address pests and diseases

Every garden will have its own set of pests and diseases – some really serious and life-threatening, others less so. Being able to identify basic pests and diseases early on in the revival process will help you make judgements as to whether a plant could or should be saved. If a perennial is smothered in sap-sucking thrips, for example, then it can be cut back and will live to see another day. However, that same pest on an established shrub could spell disaster. Check your existing plants for signs of ill-health using the following guide. You'll then be armed with enough information to allow you to make a call on treatment or removal.

DISEASES

Honey fungus

This is a soil-borne fungal disease affecting trees and shrubs. By the time it first reveals its honey-coloured mushrooms at the base of a woody plant it is already game over. This devastating disease cannot be managed, so if it is present it simply needs monitoring. Honey fungus will only affect shrubs and trees.

Phytophthora

Most common on plants growing on wet soil, this fungal disease mainly attacks woody plants. Early symptoms include dead areas on trunks and stems with dark markings under the bark. Areas of die-out in the shrub or tree are common. Monitor the plant and if necessary remove it and burn it. No chemical 'cure' is available.

Powdery mildew

This fungal disease does not necessarily cause long-term damage but it is a sign of ill health. It reveals itself as a pale grey-white powdery coating on the surface of everything from lawn grass to perennials and shrubs. Its most usual cause is dryness at the root of the plant. It can be treated with chemical fungicides and reoccurrence can be avoided with good irrigation.

Rust and black spot on roses

These two fungal diseases are the curse of the rose. They manifest themselves respectively as very obvious black spots, often with a yellow halo and orangey speckles. Both diseases can be prevented and treated with chemicals, but good cultural management, including feeding, watering and the removal of fallen leaves in autumn, will help manage the problem. Neither condition spells death for the rose.

Coral spot

This fungal disease usually enters woody plants via wounds or damage. It is most commonly spotted on dead wood but can go on to infect live tissue if left untreated. It looks like a series of rusty pimples on the surface of the bark. No treatment is available, so remove the affected timber well below the damaged area and burn the remains. Be diligent in removing diseased parts from shrubs as it easily transfers to others.

PESTS

Vine weevil

The larvae of this beetle eat through the roots of certain herbaceous species, such as heuchera, bergenia and cyclamen, while the adults nibble on the edges of leaves. Keep a close eye on vulnerable plants and treat several times a season with nematodes; these microscopic worms will kill the weevil in its larval form, thus breaking the breeding cycle.

Disorders

Mottled red or yellow markings, yellow veins, yellow leaves, brown-edged leaves and leaves with marbled markings are all signs that a plant is likely suffering from a nutrient deficiency disorder. Rectify it by using a balanced organic feed to ensure nutrients are at an optimal level. Try the RHS website for specifics on identifying the 20+ deficiency disorders. The disorder might also highlight a wider nutrient deficiency in the soil.

Aphids and other sap suckers

Usually spotted on the sappiest or newest growth of virtually any species, these insects plumb themselves into the plants' vascular system and drain it of sap. Left unchecked they can have a devastating effect. Finish off the aphids by either blasting them with water, using a fatty-acid-based pesticide or a pre-mix pesticide. Keep an eye out from early spring as they are quick to colonise plants at the start of the season.

Scale insects

These creatures barely look like insects. They have a rounded, humped outer shell (a little like a limpet) that protects them from attack while they plumb into the plant to drink its sap. They usually occur on the back of leaves and in clusters around stem junctions. There are pesticides available but it is just as efficient to remove them by hand as using chemicals can take several treatments.

Slugs and snails

Every garden is likely to have its own hoard of slugs and snails, and it is near impossible to eradicate them completely. Hand-remove them where you can, but for the greatest efficiency treat the garden with nematodes from the start of the season. This will take out a lot of the new brood and reduce subsequent breeding cycles.

Capsid bug

These insects find their way into the growing tips of shrubs and inject an anticoagulant to help the sap flow, which in turn distorts and tears the new leaves as they emerge. This pest is not always easy to spot. Affected plants should be treated with an insecticide to prevent spread and further damage.

Thrips

Once the preserve of glasshouses, thrips have become a problem outdoors thanks to warmer winters. First signs include a mottled pale pattern on the leaf surface of affected shrubs. Remove as many affected leaves as possible or use a general insecticide, targeting the back of leaves.

Suitable for Revival?

One of the challenging issues when starting the process of rejuvenating a garden is deciding what's worth reviving. Understanding at this stage the key 'vital signs' to look out for when making these decisions will save a lot of time. After all, it would be heartbreaking to spend several hours carefully pruning a shrub only to discover a few weeks later that it is suffering with honey fungus and imminent death is inevitable. Take the time to look in detail now at the plants and other existing elements of the garden. This early assessment will give you a good steer as to what is worth investing time in and what ought to be bound for the compost heap.

Many ailing plants can be brought back to good health following an initial assessment of what is making them sick.

TREES

There are a few easy steps to follow in order to make a reasonable assessment of the health of the trees in your garden. But if you do not feel confident with this a local qualified tree surgeon will be able to carry out a 'tree survey' for you, including recommended actions. Ask around for a reliable surgeon to avoid being advised to do unnecessary work. If you are going it alone, base your 'survey' on the following questions:

- Is there any die-back on the tips of the stems?

- Are there any significantly damaged branches?

- Is there sap leaking out of any wounds on the tree?

- Are there significant quantities of dead branches in the tree?

- Are there any holes in the tree or areas of rotted wood?

If the answer to any of these questions is 'yes', get a tree surgeon in to do further investigations and recommend remedial action. If the answer is 'no', it would appear the tree is in reasonable health. This then leaves you with the question: is the tree in the right place for my future plans, and what impact does it have on the garden in terms of shadow and dry soil?

See pages 63–65 for tree pruning techniques, including canopy lifting and thinning, which can reduce the shade impact of trees. See pages 23–25 for any pests or diseases you might spot.

SHRUBS

Shrubs are easier to assess than trees simply because you can see most of them up close and in detail. Many will live for decades and can be rejuvenated easily with the right pruning; others are simply short-lived and need replacing every ten years or so. Shrubs that fall into the latter category include ceanothus, sambucus, lavandula and cistus.

Assess each shrub by looking at it from every angle; from emerging stems to the leaf tips at the top. Ask yourself the following questions:

- Is there lichen growing on the shrub?

- Has more than one-third of the shrub died?

- Are there dead areas in the branches?

- Has it put on less than 2cm growth this year?

- Is there significant yellowing to the shrub (and it is not an acid-loving species)?

Significant lichen growth on trees and shrubs can indicate that the plant is no longer in active growth.

- Is there pest or disease damage that has affected more than 50 per cent of the plant?

If you answer 'yes' to one or more of these questions, the shrub in question is reasonably likely to be on its way out and ripe for removal. If all your answers are 'no', there is a good chance the shrub is in good health and suitable for a rejuvenative prune, moving or reshaping – see pages 63–65 for how to do this. And see pages 23–25 for identifying pests and diseases.

HEDGES

Hedges are often among the oldest plants in your garden. Most varieties are chosen as hedging plants in the first place because they bounce back from endless cutting, and therefore can usually be rejuvenated. Those ripe for revival include privet, holly, laurel, *Taxus* and *Thuja*, while the likes of × *Cuprocyparis leylandii*, *Chamaecyparis lawsoniana* and rosemary will not bounce back from a rejuvenative prune. It is always my feeling that the latter list of plants should be removed from the garden altogether and replaced with species that work well as hedges and can be cut as you require without fear of die-back.

The clues that your hedge may be ailing could include the following: die-back at the tips, areas of dead growth, lichen growth on stems, less than 5cm growth this year, bareness at the base, partial collapse and pest or disease damage affecting more than 50 per cent of the plant. If any of these symptoms are showing on your hedges, action is required. Pests and diseases can be treated and most hedge-appropriate plants can be cut back hard to bring them back to life and good density. See page 88 for how to rejuvenate tired hedges but consider removing × *Cuprocyparis* and *Chamaecyparis* and replacing them with *Thuja*, *Taxus*, beech or hornbeam.

CLIMBERS

Lots of vines and climbers are very long-lived. Just think of some of the knarled, woody wisteria adorning the front of stately homes. Assess your climbers by asking yourself the same questions you did for the shrubs and you'll be en route to making a reasonable health appraisal of your climbers. Lots of them can be rejuvenated (see pages 70 and 74), and see pages 23–25 for any pests or diseases you spot.

Foliage damage on perennials does not necessarily indicate long-term decline.

HERBACEOUS PERENNIALS

Perennials are fairly easy to assess. Tell-tale signs of ill health to look out for include: powdery or rusty coatings on the leaves, yellowing leaves (chlorosis), stunted or deformed growth, poor flowering and thin growth. Any of these signs could indicate that the plant is about to die, but with perennials there is usually a chance of salvation in the form of cuttings, splitting and replanting, so in most instances herbaceous plants can be saved and rejuvenated. Older clumps often die out in the middle, but this is far from game over as the plant's new growth (on its outer edge) can be lifted and replanted in the centre of the clump. See page 134 for how to revive old herbaceous plants and pages 23–25 for any pests or diseases you want to identify.

LAWNS

Poor turf is almost inevitable in a garden that has not been loved for some time. Signs that a lawn is in bad health are not hard to spot: yellowing blades, areas of die out, thin turf, excessive weeds and lots of moss indicate decline. Thankfully lawns are amongst the easiest elements of a garden to revive. See page 100 for how to bring lawn back to good fettle and page 102 for how to identify and deal with pest or diseases.

GET TO KNOW YOUR SOIL

Soil is the foundation of everything in the garden. One of the first jobs I always do on a new plot, whether it is my own or belongs to a client, is get a sense of the soil types and challenges underfoot. Take a look around the garden, as the plants can often provide a good clue as to what is happening below the surface. Plants growing well with lush foliage and good flowering can indicate a nutrient-rich soil that is moist but well drained. In contrast, spindly weak plants may indicate nutrient-poor, dry soil.

The areas plants choose to colonise of their own free will often give some clues to what is happening in the soil below. An outcrop of bog-grass (*Juncus*) is a sure sign of a waterlogged soil, whereas mass self-seeding of something like *Verbena bonariensis* may indicate a free-draining patch. Equally, a very yellow-leaved rhododendron or *Skimmia* will tell you the soil has a high pH that does not suit those plants but will be heavenly for a different group of species, such as lilacs.

The clues are all there, but to be sure it is worth having a dig around different spots on the plot. To do a really plum job, try digging a few old-fashioned 'profile pits'. These 90cm-deep trenches give the best possible insight into a soil's structure, components and type.

HOW TO CREATE A SOIL PROFILE PIT

STEP 1: Mark a square on the ground around 60 × 60cm.

STEP 2: Excavate all the soil within the square to 30cm deep.

STEP 3: Excavate half the trench down by a further 30cm.

Excavate a quarter of the trench down by a further 30cm.

STEP 5: Have a look at the soil profiles on the 90cm deep 'wall'.

Topsoil

Subsoil

Sub-subsoil

Remove fist-sized samples of topsoil, subsoil and sub-subsoil.

With all steps complete you should now have a near metre-deep hole. This will reveal the depth of the (usually brown) topsoil – ideally you'll have 20cm or more. The pit will also show how deep the next strata of the soil (subsoil) is and finally the bottom strata of sub-subsoil. You'll also be able to see if there are hard compaction pans that will affect drainage and may need addressing. It is also possible to see how much 'life' the soil has, as worms and other soil-borne creatures should be revealed. See page 98 for how to address any of the issues highlighted by the profile pit.

TESTING YOUR SOIL

With the samples of soil gathered from your profile pits, it's time to figure out which soil type you have, and therefore how to manage it or address its challenges.

Start with a golf-ball-sized lump of soil. Wet it enough so it can be formed into a ball. If it simply won't do this and the particle sizes are large and coarse, then you most likely have a sandy soil. Like any soil type, sandy soil has challenges. It will warm more quickly than most, meaning plants will often come into growth earlier, but its free-draining nature means it's likely to be dry for large portions of the year. The grittiness also means that the soil will struggle to maintain nutrients, either in it or added to it. See page 96 for how to manage this soil and make the most of it.

If the soil forms into a ball and holds together but has a matt finish when you smear your thumb across it then you likely have a silty soil. This soil type has smaller particles than sandy soil but larger than clay, meaning you sometimes have the best of both worlds. But, like any soil, it can be improved to encourage better plant health – find out how on page 96.

Finally, if the soil easily forms a ball that has a sheen to it when smeared with your thumb then it's likely clay. This form of terra firma has blessings and curses in equal measure. It is often nutrient-rich and water-retentive but can easily become waterlogged. There are also limited windows when it can be cultivated. During winter it is often wet, claggy and impossible to turn, while in summer it can bake solid and be impenetrable. Page 96 gives you a steer as to how to improve the drainage of this soil while retaining its high nutrient levels.

Soil types can be simply asserted and analysed with a soil-ball texture test.

Of course, many soils will not fit perfectly into one of the three types mentioned. But armed with the basic principles of identification you should be able to assess if you have a silty clay, a stoney clay or a 50:50 sand-silt mix.

With soil samples to hand it's also worth assessing the pH levels. This is simply the relative acidity or alkalinity of the soil. Again, the plants already in the garden may give you clues. If the whole plot is planted with rhododendrons, camellias, ericas and kalmias then it is likely an acid soil. If a few of these plants are present but looking a little yellow and tired, you possibly have a neutral soil. And, of course, if none are present then it either means that the soil is alkaline or previous gardeners had a dislike of acid-loving plants. To be sure, buy a small soil pH testing kit from the garden centre or online. The test process is little more than adding your soil and a few compounds to a glass tube, sealing it, then shaking the bejesus out of it. The contents of the tube will settle, revealing a colour. Simply compare this to the chart provided to get your soil pH reading.

If you can muster the effort it is worthwhile digging a few profile pits as the soil type and pH can change across a relatively small site depending on how it has been managed in the past. Armed with all this information about your soil you are ready to make decisions as to how you might improve it or which plants are naturally likely to thrive in it. See page 98 for how to improve your soil.

Identifying existing plants and how to manage them

An established garden is, more often than not, full to the gunnels with existing plants. Some of them may be useful and worth retaining, others may be brought back to life with a radical prune, while certain among them are not worth the bother. Before you can decide what to keep, improve or remove it's vital that you can identify what you've been blessed or cursed with. Here I've compiled a list of the 100 plants you are most likely to find in established gardens. These are generally the sorts of species that thrive in spite of a lack of attention and therefore have been able to survive the garden's slide into neglect. Many are worth keeping, or moving in their existing states, while others can be radically improved with pruning or by having other plants added to them. Use this guide to spot what you've got and then decide on whether those plants fit into your new vision for the garden in either their existing state or with a revival improvement.

*Plant sizes, colours and forms are based on the most common cultivar of that plant.

SHRUBS

AUCUBA

H/S: 3 × 3m

Interest: Evergreen mottled foliage.

What can you do with it?: Dig it out and replace it with something nicer! Topiarise it (see page 84). Hedge it (see page 88). Move it (see page 132).

BERBERIS

H/S: 2 × 1.5m

Interest: Evergreen/deciduous. Spiny. Burgundy/green foliage. Yellow/orange flowers in spring.

What can you do with it?: Rejuvenate it (see page 63). Grow a climber through it (see page 144). Grow plants underneath it (see page 164).

BUDDLEJA

H/S: 3 × 2 + m

Interest: Deciduous shrub. Spring/summer spikes of flowers. Loved by butterflies. Self-seeds.

What can you do with it?: Rejuvenate it (see page 63). Grow climbers through it (see page 144). Grow underneath it (see page 164).

BUXUS

H/S: 3 × 2m

Interest: Reliable small-leaved evergreen. It has a growth spurt in spring.

What can you do with it?: Topiarise it (see page 84). Hedge it (see page 88). Lift the canopy for large specimens (see page 65). Move it (see page 132).

CAMELLIA

H/S: 3 × 2m

Interest: Large white, red and pink flowers in winter/spring. Evergreen.

What can you do with it?: Replace it with a better plant! Rejuvenate it (see page 63).

CEANOTHUS

H/S: 3 × 3m

Interest: Intense blue flowers in late spring. Evergreen. Short-lived.

What can you do with it?: Grow a climber through it (see page 144). Grow plants underneath it (see page 164).

SHRUBS

CHOISYA

H/S: 1.2 × 1.2m

Interest: Evergreen gold or green foliage. Scented foliage. White flowers in spring.

What can you do with it?: Move it (see page 132). Rejuvenate it (see page 63). Topiarise it (see page 84).

CORNUS SIBERICA

H/S: 1 × 1m (with annual prune)

Interest: Bright orange, red and yellow stems in winter. Green or variegated foliage.

What can you do with it?: Hard prune annually (see page 85). Move it (see page 132).

COTINUS

H/S: 3 × 2m

Interest: Deciduous shrub. Smokey-looking flowers in summer. Rounded burgundy foliage.

What can you do with it?: Rejuvenate it (see page 63). Grow a climber through it (see page 144). Grow underneath it (see page 164).

COTONEASTER

H/S: 2 × 2m (very variable, dependent on species)

Interest: Semi-evergreen. White flowers in spring. Autumn berries.

What can you do with it?: Rejuvenate it (see page 63). Plant through it (see page 144).

ELAEAGNUS

H/S: 3 × 2m

Interest: Evergreen silver-green or variegated foliage. Insignificant scented winter flowers.

What can you do with it?: Hedge it (see page 88). Move it (see page 132). Grow through it (see page 144).

ESCALLONIA

H/S: 2 × 2m+

Interest: Evergreen shrub. Small pink, white or red spring flowers. Some forms scented.

What can you do with it?: Rejuvenate it (see page 63). Grow climbers through it (see page 144). Grow underneath it (see page 164). Hedge it (see page 88).

SHRUBS

EUONYMUS JAPONICUS

H/S: 1 × 1m

Interest: Evergreen. A reliable shrub. Usually pest-free.

What can you do with it?: Hedge it (see page 88). Topiarise it (see page 84). Move it (see page 132).

EUPHORBIA (shrubby)

H/S: 1 × 1m

Interest: Bright green spikes of flowers in spring. Evergreen foliage.

What can you do with it?: Move it (see page 132). Rejuvenate it (see page 63).

FORSYTHIA

H/S: 2.5 × 2m

Interest: Bright yellow flowers for 3 months in spring. Plain deciduous foliage. Vase form.

What can you do with it?: Thin in spring (see page 64). Grow plants underneath it (see page 164). Grow a climber through it (see page 144).

FUCHSIA (HARDY)

H/S: 1.5 × 1.5m

Interest: Deciduous shrub. Red and purple flowers from late spring to autumn.

What can you do with it?: Move it (see page 132). Rejuvenate it (see page 63). Grow underneath it (see page 164).

HEBE

H/S: 1.5 × 1.5m

Interest: Blue, white and pink flowers in summer and autumn. Evergreen foliage.

What can you do with it?: Move it (see page 132). Rejuvenate it (see page 63).

HYDRANGEA

H/S: 1.5 × 1.5m

Interest: Large flowers from mid-summer to autumn. Large leaves.

What can you do with it?: Revival pruning (see page 63). Grow plants underneath it (see page 164). Dry the flower heads.

SHRUBS

HYPERICUM (SHRUBBY)

H/S: 1.5 × 1.5m

Interest: Yellow flowers in summer.

What can you do with it?: Move it (see page 132). Grow through it (see page 144).

ILEX

H/S: 5 × 5m+

Interest: Glossy evergreen foliage. Red berries in autumn and winter.

What can you do with it?: Hedge it (see page 88). Topiarise it (see page 84). Grow a climber through it (see page 144). Revive it (see page 63). Thin the canopy (see page 65).

KERRIA

H/S: 3 × 1m

Interest: Vase form. Yellow button-shaped flowers in spring.

What can you do with it?: Rejuvenate it (see page 64). Move it (see page 132).

LAURUS NOBILIS

H/S: 6 × 4m+

Interest: Scented evergreen foliage.

What can you do with it?: Hedge it (see page 88). Topiarise it (see page 84). Rejuvenate it (see page 63).

LAVANDULA

H/S: 60 × 60cm

Interest: Evergreen. Scented flowers and foliage in summer.

What can you do with it?: Clip it and refresh it (see page 84). Move it (see page 132).

LAVATERA

H/S: 2.5 × 1.5m

Interest: Large pink or white flowers in summer.

What can you do with it?: Rejuvenate it (see page 63). Grow plants underneath it (see page 164). Use as a quick screen (see page 177).

SHRUBS

LIGUSTRUM

H/S: 3 × 2.5m

Interest: Evergreen shrub and hedging plant. Small white flowers in late Spring/Summer.

What can you do with it?: Hedge it (see page 88). Topiarise it (see page 84). Rejuvenate it (see page 63).

LONICERA

H/S: 1.5 × 1.5m

Interest: Evergreen gold foliage.

What can you do with it?: Topiarise it (see page 84). Move it (see page 132). Grow a climber over it (see page 144).

MAGNOLIA

H/S: 4 × 4m+

Interest: Large white, burgundy, yellow and pink flowers in spring. Deciduous foliage.

What can you do with it?: Lift the canopy (see page 65). Grow plants underneath it (see page 164).

MAHONIA JAPONICA

H/S: 2 × 2m

Interest: Scented yellow flowers in winter. Evergreen. Pest free.

What can you do with it?: Pruning not required but the canopy can be lifted, Grow an annual climber through it or Move it (see pages 65, 144, 132).

OSMANTHUS

H/S: 2 × 2m

Interest: Scented flowers in winter. Evergreen foliage.

What can you do with it?: Hedge it (see page 88). Topiarise it (see page 84). Move it (see page 132).

PHILADELPHUS

H/S: 2.5 × 2m

Interest: Shrub. Scented white flowers in late spring. Deciduous.

What can you do with it?: Thin in spring (see page 64). Grow plants underneath it (see page 164).

SHRUBS

POTENTILLA (SHRUBBY)
H/S: 70 × 70cm
Interest: Long-flowering from late spring to autumn. White, red, orange or yellow flowers.
What can you do with it?: Move it (see page 132).

PYRACANTHA
H/S: 3 × 3m+
Interest: White flowers in spring followed by summer/autumn berries. Evergreen. A wall shrub.
What can you do with it?: Grow a climber through it (see page 144). Hedge it (see page 88). Revive it (see page 63).

PHOTINIA
H/S: 3 × 3m
Interest: Red leaves in spring. White flowers in spring/summer. Evergreen. A hedge plant.
What can you do with it?: Rejuvenate it (see page 63). Move it (see page 132). Grow a climber through it (see page 144).

SHRUBS

RHODODENDRON

H/S: 2 × 2m +

Interest: Deciduous or evergreen shrub. Bright spring flowers. Prefers acid soil. Some forms scented.

What can you do with it?: Rejuvenate it (see page 63). Grow climbers through it (see page 144). Grow underneath it (see page 164)

RIBES

H/S: 2 × 1.5m

Interest: Pink, red or white flowers in spring. Vase form. Some berries.

What can you do with it?: Thin in spring (see page 88). Grow plants underneath it (see page 164). Grow a climber through it (see page 144).

SHRUBS

ROSA
H/S: 2 × 1.5m
Interest: Large flowers from early summer to autumn. Deciduous foliage. Some are scented.
What can you do with it?: Rejuvenate it (see page 164). Grow plants underneath it (see page 88). Use as cut flowers.

SKIMMIA
H/S: 1.5 ×.1.5m
Interest: Evergreen shrub. Winter berries. Spring flowers.
What can you do with it?: Move it (see page 132).

SPIRAEA
H/S: 1.5 × 1.5m
Interest: Deciduous shrub. Clusters of white, red and pink flowers in early summer.
What can you do with it?: Rejuvenate it (see page 63). Move it (see page 132). Grow a climber through it (see page 144).

SYRINGA
H/S: 3 × 2m
Interest: Deciduous shrub. Scented white, pink, blue or lilac flowers in summer.
What can you do with it?: Lift the canopy (see page 65). Grow underneath it (see page 164).

VINCA
H/S: 40cm × infinite
Interest: Blue and mauve flowers in spring. Evergreen foliage. Groundcovering. Spreading.
What can you do with it?: Crop it over to rejuvenate it. Plant bulbs through it (see page 148). Move it (see page 132).

WEIGELA
H/S: 2 × 2m
Interest: White, pink or red flowers in early summer.
What can you do with it?: Move it (see page 132).

CLIMBERS

CLEMATIS
H/S: 3 × 3m+

Interest: Red, pink, blue, white or purple flowers – all seasons depending on species.

What can you do with it?: Rejuvenate it (see page 63). Prune it (see page 87). Grow another climber through it (see page 144).

HEDERA
H/S: 5 × 5m+

Interest: Evergreen foliage. Flowers and berries in autumn/winter. Adventitious roots.

What can you do with it?: Rejuvenate it (see page 63). Grow another climber through it (see page 144). Remove it.

JASMINUM
H/S: 3 × 3m

Interest: Yellow or white flowers in winter/summer respectively. A scandent/twining climber.

What can you do with it?: Rejuvenate it (see page 63). Move it (see page 132).

CLIMBERS

PARTHENOCISSUS

H/S: 10m +

Interest: Deciduous self-clinging climber. Bright red autumn foliage. Best in full sun.

What can you do with it?: Rejuvenate it (see page 63). Grow other climbers through it (see page 144). Grow underneath it (see page 164).

WISTERIA

H/S: 5 × 5m+

Interest: Racemes of lilac, purple, pink, white flowers in spring. Twining stems.

What can you do with it?: Rejuvenate it (see page 63). Prune it (see page 74). Grow plants underneath it (see page 164). Grow another climber through it (see page 144).

LONICERA

H/S: 3 × 3m

Interest: Scented cream and pink summer flowers. Some species are semi-evergreen.

What can you do with it?: Grow another climber through it (see page 144). Rejuvenate it (see page 63).

ALCHEMILLA MOLLIS

H/S: 40 × 40cm

Interest: Lime flowers and scalloped foliage.

What can you do with it?: Split and replant it (see page 134). Grow other plants through it (see page 144).

ANEMONE JAPONICA

H/S: 1m × 50cm

Interest: Pink, white or burgundy flowers in late summer/autumn.

What can you do with it?: Split and replant it (see page 134). Plant bulbs through it (see page 148).

ACHILLEA

H/S: 50 × 50cm

Interest: Flat plates of red, yellow, orange, white or pink flowers through summer.

What can you do with it?: Split and replant it (see page 134).

AQUILEGIA
H/S: 50 × 40cm
Interest: Nodding flowers in every colour in late spring and early summer.
What can you do with it?: Move it (see page 132). Collect and sow seeds (see page 138).

HERBACEOUS PERENNIALS AND BULBS

ASPLENIUM

H/S: 40 × 40cm

Interest: Evergreen fern.

What can you do with it?: Split and replant it (see page 134).

ASTER

H/S: 20cm–2m × 40cm–1m

Interest: White, pink, blue, purple or violet daisy-like flowers in late summer and autumn.

What can you do with it?: Split and replant it (see page 134).

BERGENIA

H/S: 40cm × 2m+

Interest: Large glossy evergreen leaves. Pink, white and red flowers in spring.

What can you do with it?: Split and replant it (see page 134). Plant bulbs through it (see page 148).

BORAGO

H/S: 60 × 60cm

Interest: Blue flowers in spring and summer. Coarse deciduous foliage.

What can you do with it?: Move it (see page 132). Collect and sow seeds (see page 138).

CAMPANULA (TALL)

H/S: 1.2 × 1m

Interest: Bell-shaped white, blue, mauve, purple and pink flowers in summer.

What can you do with it?: Split and replant it (see page 134).

CENTAUREA

H/S: 50 × 50cm

Interest: Blue, purple and white flowers in late spring/early summer.

What can you do with it?: Split and replant it (see page 134). Collect and sow seeds (see page 138).

HERBACEOUS PERENNIALS AND BULBS

DICENTRA

H/S: 50 × 50cm

Interest: Pink and white heart-shaped flowers in late spring.

What can you do with it?: Grow other plants through it (see page 144). Plant bulbs through it (see page 148). Move it (see page 132).

DIGITALIS

H/S: 1m × 40cm

Interest: Spikes of pink, purple and white flowers in spring/summer. Biennial.

What can you do with it?: Collect and sow seeds (see page 138).

CONVALLARIA

H/S: 25 × 50cm+

Interest: Highly scented white flowers in spring.

What can you do with it?: Grow other plants through it (see page 144). Split and replant it (see page 134).

HERBACEOUS PERENNIALS AND BULBS

ECHINOPS

H/S: 1.5 × 1m

Interest: Balls of spiky blue flowers through summer.

What can you do with it?: Split and replant it (see page 134). Grow an annual climber through it (see page 144).

GALANTHUS

H/S: 20 × 20cm

Interest: White flowers in late winter.

What can you do with it?: Split and replant it (see page134). Grow other plants through it (see page 144).

GERANIUM

H/S: 50 × 70cm

Interest: White, blue, pink or mauve flowers through spring and summer.

What can you do with it?: Split and replant it (see page 134). Plant bulbs through it (see page 148).

GEUM

H/S: 40 × 40cm

Interest: Red, yellow, orange or cream flowers in late spring and summer.

What can you do with it?: Split and replant it (see page 134). Move it (see page 132).

HELENIUM

H/S: 1 × 1m

Interest: Red and yellow daisy-like flowers in late summer and autumn.

What can you do with it?: Split and replant it (see page 134). Give it a Chelsea chop.

HELLEBORUS

H/S: 40 × 40cm

Interest: Pink, red, burgundy or white rose-like flowers in early spring

What can you do with it?: Split and replant it (see page 134). Plant late bulbs through it (see page 148).

HEUCHERA

H/S: 60 × 40cm

Interest: Evergreen foliage in tones from burgundy to lime green. Spikes of white flowers in spring.

What can you do with it?: Move it (see page 132).

HOSTA

H/S: 50 × 40cm+

Interest: Lush foliage in rounded hummocks. Mauve or white flowers in summer.

What can you do with it?: Split and replant it (see page 134). Move it (see page 132).

HYACINTHOIDES NON-SCRIPTA

H/S: 30 × 30cm

Interest: Blue bell-shaped flowers in spring. Naturalises. UK native.

What can you do with it?: Split and replant it (see page 134). Collect and sow seeds (see page 138).

MELISSA

H/S: 50 × 50cm

Interest: Lemon-scented leaves and small white flowers.

What can you do with it?: Collect and sow seeds (see page 138). Move it (see page 132).

LAMIUM

H/S: 30cm × infinite

Interest: Year-round variegated foliage. Pink, white or yellow flowers.

What can you do with it?: Move it (see page 132). Split and replant it (see page 134).

IRIS (BEARDED)

H/S: 70 × 40cm

Interest: Large flowers in every colour in late spring/early summer.

What can you do with it?: Split and replant it (see page 134). Plant bulbs through it (see page 148).

HERBACEOUS PERENNIALS AND BULBS

MENTHA

H/S: 60cm × infinite

Interest: Herb. Little aesthetic interest.

What can you do with it?: Split and replant it(see page 134).

MUSCARI

H/S: 30 × 30cm

Interest: Bulb. Blue grape-like flowers in spring.

What can you do with it?: Collect and sow seeds (see page 138). Move it (see page 132).

NEPETA

H/S: 30 × 70cm

Interest: Silvery foliage. Pale blue flowers through summer.

What can you do with it?: Plant bulbs through it (see page 148). Split and replant it (see page 134).

LYSIMACHIA

H/S: 50 × 50cm

Interest: Yellow flowers in summer.

What can you do with it?: Split and replant it (see page 134). Grow it in long grass (see page 155).

NARCISSUS

H/S: 40 × 40cm

Interest: Yellow flowers in spring.

What can you do with it?: Grow it in long grass (see page 155). Move it (see page 132).

ORIGANUM

H/S: 40 × 50cm

Interest: Herb. Pink flowers in summer. Great for pollinators.

What can you do with it?: Split and replant it (see page 134).

PAEONIA

H/S: 50 × 60cm

Interest: Large cupped flowers in pink, white, red or burgundy.

What can you do with it?: Move it – yes you can! (see page 132).

PAPAVER

H/S: 1m × 40cm

Interest: Large red, white, burgundy, mauve or pink flowers in early summer.

What can you do with it?: Collect and sow seeds (see page 138). Split and replant it (see page 134).

PENSTEMON

H/S: 70 × 70cm

Interest: Pendulous bell-shaped flowers in every colour from summer to autumn.

What can you do with it?: Move it (see page 132).

HERBACEOUS PERENNIALS AND BULBS

PHLOX

H/S: 80 × 80cm

Interest: Clusters of pink, white, blue, mauve and red flowers through summer.

What can you do with it?: Split and replant it (see page 134).

PULMONARIA

H/S: 30 × 40cm

Interest: Mottled leaves. Pink, blue, red or white flowers in early spring.

What can you do with it?: Move it (see page 132). Split and replant it (see page 134).

RUDBECKIA

H/S: 70 × 50cm

Interest: Large yellow or orange daisy-like flowers through summer and autumn.

What can you do with it?: Split and replant it (see page 134).

SALVIA (SHRUBBY SAGE)

H/S: 1.2 × 1.2m

Interest: Red, white, yellow, pink, blue and purple flowers from summer to autumn.

What can you do with it?: Rejuvenate it (see page 63). Grow plants through it (see page 144).

SEDUM

H/S: 50 × 50cm

Interest: Year-round foliage. Red, white or pink flowers in summer. The flowers are attractive to insects.

What can you do with it?: Split and replant it (see page 134).

SOLIDAGO

H/S: 1.2 × 1m

Interest: Plumes of yellow flowers in summer.

What can you do with it?: Split and replant it (see page 134).

TREES

ACER JAPANESE

H/S: 3 × 3m+

Interest: Burgundy, green or yellow leaves. Good autumn foliage colour.

What can you do with it?: Move it (see page 132). Grow plants underneath it (see page 164).

ACER PSEUDOPLATANUS

H/S: 7 × 5m

Interest: Little interest.

What can you do with it?: Remove it and replace with an attractive tree!

BETULA

H/S: 10 × 5m+

Interest: White bark.

What can you do with it?: Reshape it (see page 64). Grow a climber through it (see page 144). Thin the canopy (see page 64).

TREES

CHAMAECYPARIS

H/S: 5 × 3m+

Interest: Conifer. Evergreen with gold, grey or green foliage.

What can you do with it?: Grow a climber through it (see page 144). Remove it!

X CUPROCYPARIS LEYLANDII

H/S: 7 × 3m+

Interest: Hedge. Evergreen. No interest.

What can you do with it?: Remove it and replace with Thuja or Taxus!

FRAXINUS EXCELSIOR

H/S: 7 × 4m+

Interest: Pinnate leaves. No interest.

What can you do with it?: Remove it and replace with an attractive tree!

CRATAEGUS

H/S: 6 × 6m+

Interest: White, red or pink flowers in spring. Summer/autumn berries.

What can you do with it?: Rejuvenate it (see page 63). Hedge it (see page 88).

MALUS (CRAB APPLE)

H/S: 4.5 × 4.5m

Interest: White, pink or burgundy flowers in spring. Fruit from mid-summer.

What can you do with it?: Grow a climber through it (see page 144). Grow plants underneath it (see page 164). Thin the canopy (see page 64).

PRUNUS AVIUM

H/S: 7 × 4m+

Interest: Small white flowers in spring.

What can you do with it?: Remove it and replace with an attractive cherry!

PRUNUS (JAPANESE)
H/S: Extremely variable.
Interest: White or pink blossom
in spring.
What can you do with it?:
Reshape it (see page 64).
Grow plants underneath it
(see page 164). Thin the
canopy (see page 64).

TREES

SORBUS
H/S: 6 × 3m+
Interest: White flowers in spring. Autumn berries.
What can you do with it?: Reshape it (see page 64). Grow plants underneath it (see page 164).

TAXUS
H/S: 10 × 5m+
Interest: Evergreen hedge plant.
What can you do with it?: Topiarise it (see page 84). Move it (see page 132). Hedge it (see page 88). Rejuvenate it (see page 63).

PYRUS
H/S: 4 × 3m+
Interest: White flowers in spring. Fruit from summer to autumn.
What can you do with it?: Rejuvenate it (see page 63). Grow plants underneath it (see page 164). Lift the canopy (see page 65).

prune

Pruning is central to rejuvenating a garden. With the right techniques it's possible to breathe life back into woody plants that are no longer at their best. An initial assessment of your garden will have highlighted the shrubs and trees ripe for revival, as well as those beyond redemption. Some saveable plants may simply require dead and diseased stems removing, while others will need a total reshape or a fundamental change to their structure. Before launching into a full-scale hack, it's worth thinking about the why, when and how of the process. For every one of your pruning actions there will be a reaction from the plant. Arming yourself with the knowledge of how they will respond to what you do will give you confidence that every cut is going to trigger the outcome you want.

Why prune?

The focus of this book is rejuvenation and reshaping pruning, but gardeners have traditionally cut bits off plants for all sorts of reasons. Often it is to improve display and yield with pruning techniques developed to maximise fruit and flower production. But pruning is also used to change the shape and habit of plants, to control their size, to topiarise them and to change their behaviour. For example, left to its own devices a *Cotinus coggygria* will produce a mass of leaves the size of ping-pong balls and a smokey fuzz of flowers. However, it becomes quite a different plant if it is hard pruned in spring: the leaf size doubles or triples and it doesn't flower. Alternatively, the same plant can be clipped on its sides, producing a hedge-like effect topped with smokey-looking blooms, or it can have its lower canopy cleared of side stems to reveal clean branches some 2m tall with a mass of growth on top. Therefore, how and when you prune a plant, along with the frequency, will create fundamentally different effects.

Rejuvenation pruning often involves removing branches to soil level in order to trigger basal dormant buds into growth.

How plants respond to different types of pruning

Most woody plants are driven by what is known as apical dominance. This means that the leading or dominant shoot (usually the tallest) is where the plant is focusing its energies on cell division and therefore growth. Pruning off this dominant shoot makes the plant refocus its hormones and growth to the first set of buds below the cut. These buds will now receive hormones, triggering their growth and effectively turning them into a pair of dominant shoots. If after a year these new shoots are pruned back, the buds below each one will receive hormones and therefore be triggered into growth.

This naturally occurring process can be employed by us gardeners to alter the way a plant is growing. Simply trimming a hedge will trigger this effect, causing the individual plants to gradually thicken up, growth and an improvement in the density of the hedge. Equally, an individual shrub can be encouraged to produce multiple side stems by removing the dominant apical leader.

Another phenomenon caused by pruning is the emergence of dormant buds. By carrying out a hard cut-back, which many shrubs requiring rejuvenation need, you will often be cutting into old woody trunks with no sign of leaf or life. However, tucked under the bark of many species are dormant buds. These are evident when rejuvenating a camellia, for example. A trunk reduced from 3m to 1m will start to generate what appears to be a series of nobbles or warts below the cut. These are the beginnings of the dormant buds sparking into life. Essentially, pruning has forced the plant to redirect its energies and hormones to this old wood, thus breathing life into potential buds that have been lurking under there.

For some species a hard-prune will trigger dormant buds into growth.

Dormant buds under the bark of some trees and shrubs will be triggered into growth by pruning.

When should you prune?

The question of when to cut bits off a plant is both complex and very straightforward. The easy answer to this question is: 'after flowering'. This approach, which of course has exceptions, is the safest bet if you are unsure of when to tackle a wayward *Weigela* or a top-heavy *Tamarix*. The 'prune-after-flowering' principle is simply based on the fact that some plants flower on stems they've produced in the current year, while others bloom on stems that grew in the previous year. A good example of this is rambling and climbing roses. Most rambling roses produce flowers on the stems they grew in the previous year. So if you hard-prune a rambling rose in spring you'll be cutting off its flowering stems, leaving you bereft of blooms in summer. Delay the

pruning until after the rambler has flowered in early summer and it will have time to make new stems before autumn, which will go on to flower the next year. Climbing roses are different in that they produce flowers on the stems they grow in the current year. This means you can hard-prune them in spring and the resulting stems will make flowers in the same year. Of course, if you get this wrong with roses the worst likely outcome is that you simply have one flower-free year. But with other plants, pruning at the wrong time can have dire consequences. Say, for example, you hard prune a shrub back to structural branches in early autumn. There will be enough warmth still that the plant will probably make tentative new stems and leaves but they will

have no time to ripen or harden up ready for winter, meaning they will likely be killed by the first frost. This in turn may cause the plant to kick the bucket altogether.

Pruning times are not just driven by ensuring good flowering, though. Apples are traditionally pruned in mid-winter, while their close relative, cherries, are only pruned in summer. This is because of diseases that will potentially affect the trees if they are left with open wounds in the wrong season. And hedges are a whole other matter. Ideally they should be left alone until at least mid-summer to prevent disturbing nesting birds. But fear not, follow the pruning guidelines here and you'll have healthy plants in good shape that bloom on cue.

WHERE TO CUT

Plants require slightly different approaches when it comes to their individual pruning but the ideal point at which to make a cut on any branch, twig or stem is consistent. Cut too close to the bud and it will be unable to produce a leaf, stem or flower. Cut too far away and you are left with what is known as a 'snag' or uncut twig above a bud, which is likely to rot or become victim to fungal attack. Ideally, aim to make pruning cuts around 5–10mm above a bud or node. A slight angle will help prevent water sitting on top of a cut stem, which can lead to rotting or fungal ingress.

The ideal pruning cut should be just above a bud.

Key pruning types

The are numerous styles and approaches to pruning but the methods you'll need to use when reviving your garden and maintaining it afterwards can be summarised as: rejuvenative pruning, reshaping pruning, productivity pruning and cyclical pruning. They each suit different plants and will deliver different outcomes. Before you attempt any of these methods there is a generic process that every species needs to go through before getting its specialist prune. This generic process is the initial removal of dead, diseased and damaged wood. It is often referred to as the three Ds. And I might add a 'C' to the end of the acronym to equal the removal of crossing wood, in other words, branches rubbing against one another.

green or pale and wet then the stem is alive; if it is black or brown then the stem is likely dead. Make neat cuts (see above) and dispose of any diseased material by burning. Other branches that show early signs of disease, such as the small orange pustules of coral spot (see page 24), should also be removed and burned. Branches that are damaged, torn or snapped can also be cut off. Finally, look out for any crossing branches that are either compromising the form of the shrub or rubbing against other branches, and remove them.

With the three Ds + C addressed you are now ready to carry out the rest of the prune, be that rejuvenative, shaping or productivity led.

Hard pruning the stems of some mature woody plants can initiate new growth.

BEFORE YOU START A SPECIALIST PRUNE

Give any tree or shrub you are planning to work on a good assessment from every angle possible before you begin. Start by removing the dead wood. This is easier in summer as dead stems are more evident due to their lack of leaves. If you are unsure, make a tiny scrape on the bark with your secateurs. If the colour underneath is either

REJUVENATIVE PRUNING

This form of pruning is likely to make up the lion's share of the work you will be doing in the revival garden. Unlike cyclical pruning, it is a more radical approach that sees mature shrubs cut back to their bare structural bones or even to the ground. See page 85 for all the shrubs that can be rejuvenated in this way, and how to do it.

RESHAPING PRUNING

Some plants in the revival garden may be in perfect health and in the right place but are just not quite the right shape. A plant may be too wide, too tall or too dense, or it may be taking up lots of ground space that could be otherwise planted.

Crown reduction

A plant's overall scale can be reduced with a crown reduction. This process involves making the leafy canopy smaller by cutting it back by up to 40 per cent across the whole surface. The idea is to end up with a natural-looking plant that just has a smaller canopy. Avoid the supermarket-car-park planting look by following the natural form of the plant and not trimming it into an odd topiarised blob on a stick (see page 192).

Aim for a natural rather than manicured look when reshaping shrubs.

Crown thinning

If the plant is the right shape and size but is compromising other plants around it due to its dense canopy blocking the light, the answer is a crown thin. The idea of this technique is to create natural-looking gaps or holes through the crown by judiciously removing stems and branches in the upper canopy of the shrub or tree. A thin-out of 30–40 per cent will have little ill-effect on the plant in question but will make a huge difference to light levels beneath it. The process will need repeating every few years to prevent the canopy 'closing up' again.

Effectively cutting holes through a mature shrub will allow more plants to grow beneath it.

Crown lifting

Crown lifting is another useful pruning technique in the revival garden. It can be applied to shrubs and trees and simply involves removing lower stems, branches and growth. The idea is to leave the shrubs or tree with bare branches or trunk up to 2m high with foliage only allowed to grow above this point. It's a useful way to get more light onto the ground, open up soil space for planting and to create new views and vistas through the garden.

PRODUCTIVITY PRUNING

This form of pruning can be summarised as the work you need to do every year to keep plants in good health, shape and performance. A suitable example would be *Cornus sanguinea*. If it is not pruned every spring it loses the red stems it is grown for, thus providing little value to the garden. Many plants, from topiary to shrubs, trees and hedges, need annual pruning of one description or another to keep them performing well. Again, *The Pruning of Trees, Shrubs and Conifers* is the place to seek this information.

ON-GOING PRUNING

Once you have revived shrubs and trees in your garden, subsequent years will call for various pruning techniques to ensure good production of flowers, fruit or foliage. Different species require very different approaches to keep them in regular productivity. For example, Hybrid Tea roses will slowly reduce their number of flowers over several seasons if they are not hard-pruned in spring each year. This broad and complex subject is covered well in the iconic pruning bible: *The Pruning of Trees, Shrubs and Conifers* by George E Brown and Tony Kirkham. It's the equivalent of *The Catcher in the Rye* for the horticultural world and is a book no gardener should be without.

PRUNING KIT

Once you've revived your garden there will be ongoing pruning work to keep it in good nick, so it's worth investing in some good-quality gear. Secateurs are perhaps the most important tool in your armoury. Anvil types are not suited to several forms of pruning, so go for bypass secateurs. Both Niwaki and Felco produce high-quality versions of these, along with the all-important holster so they are always at your side. The other essential bit of kit is a sturdy pruning saw. The fold-up forms are the most practical as they are light, small, devilishly sharp and easily fit into a back pocket. Complete your pruning cache with loppers and a bowsaw. Often the best loppers are those with very long or extendable handles for extra leverage. As for the bowsaw, the bigger the better as it will be called upon for heavier trunks.

Tree Preservation Orders: Before doing any work in your garden check with the local authority's Tree Preservation Officer if there's a Tree Preservation Order (TPO) on any of your trees. Ignoring a TPO by pruning, removing or altering the soil level around a tree by more than 200mm can land you with a fine of £60,000!

Disposal of arisings: Pruning work inevitably generates lots of cut branches and stems. There are a number of ways to deal with them. Some local authorities will take them at waste sites or they may be able to be cut up and placed in the garden waste bin. If you are generating large quantities then consider hiring a petrol chipper. These machines can turn branches up to 50mm in diameter into 2 × 2cm chips, radically reducing their volume in the process. The chips will need to be stored for a year or so before they can be used in the garden as mulch or for path surfaces. This is because freshly chipped wood will suck nitrogen out of the soil. Also consider holding onto finer stems and twigs that can be used as 'pea sticks' to support herbaceous plants.

Hiring a tree surgeon: Some pruning jobs are just too big, too high up or too dangerous to tackle yourself, so you'll require the services of an arboriculturalist. Use the Arboricultural Association or other professional bodies to find a fully qualified, experienced and insured tree surgeon in your area.

Pruning basics

The basic principles applied to cutting stems, branches and trunks are the same.

STEP 1: Reduce the weight of the branch by making an under cut, followed by a top cut 50cm+ from where you want the final cut to be. This process prevents any tearing of bark, which can have difficulty healing, and takes the weight out of the branch so there is no risk of tearing when you make the final cut.

STEP 2: Identify the collar of the branch, where it emerges from the tree, and make an angled cut underneath the branch. This eliminates any chance of the bark tearing as you make the final finished cut.

STEP 3: Make an angled cut down from the top of the branch to join your under cut.

STEP 4: You should be left with a clean cut sloping away from the tree, which will prevent the ingress of water and fungal diseases. Don't be tempted to use a 'wound sealant' – at best they do nothing, at worst they actually seal in fungal problems.

Good callusing from an historic pruning cut.

Common Roses

Roses are among the most misunderstood plants when it comes to pruning. All too often they are given tentative prunes year after year, leading them to become ugly leggy monsters with a metre of bare, knarled thorny stems topped with the lightest toupee of foliage and the occasional flower. Thankfully most of these poor tortured creatures can be brought back to life with relative ease.

The approach I apply is fairly drastic, but in my experience it works really well 96.2 per cent of the time! And it needn't be restricted to Hybrid Tea and Floribunda roses, it can be used for the most common roses you are likely to encounter in your revival garden, these being English, Patio and Polyantha. A rejuvenative prune to any of these forms has the potential to trigger new growths from the base, which will turn the rose back into a full, bushy, floriferous, rounded and healthy plant.

Reviving other roses

Species roses and old roses such as Damask, Gallica, Bourbon, China, Alba and Musk will not take to such a radical rejuvenative prune. Instead, ailing specimens of these roses should have all their oldest growths cut to the ground, leaving up to one-third of the plant intact but composed solely of its youngest (1–2 years) stems. (See page 70 for how to do a rejuvenative prune on climbing and rambling roses.)

REJUVENATING HYBRID TEA ROSES

STEP 1: Assess the rose. Ideally it will have multiple actively growing stems emerging from the base that are fully clothed in leaves. If this is the case then the rose need only be pruned in spring to reduce its overall height by half, aiming to achieve a goblet-shaped plant, and only pruned to outward-facing buds. If, however, the rose is a mass of bare stems and little top growth you'll need to do a rejuvenative prune.

STEP 2: To carry out a rejuvenative prune, start by removing the bulky branches of the rose, using either a handsaw, loppers or secateurs, down to around 30cm in early spring. The resulting plant is now likely to be a series of leafless stumps but don't let this worry you. Using the same tools, make your final cuts down to around 10cm from the ground. Aim to cut just above nodes or dormant buds that are facing out from the centre of the rose.

STEP 3: Roses are gross feeders, meaning they greedily consume high levels of nutrients from the soil. This revival prune will trigger lots of new growth that will be hungrier than ever, so it's important to feed directly after pruning. A balanced organic slow-release feed applied to the soil surface will do the trick, along with a heavy manure mulch and season-long feeding, both to the roots and foliage, with liquid seaweed.

Climbing roses

I find climbing roses the most gratifying of all plants to revive. With the right pruning a scrappy, tangled, flower-free mess can be turned into a floriferous well-structured plant in under four months. These step-by-step instructions highlight the process and outcomes you should expect.

REJUVENATING CLIMBING ROSES

STEP 1: Start with the usual removal of dead, diseased and damaged stems, along with any that are crossing one another. Leave the rose attached to the wall or fence for this part of the process so you can assess which stems to preserve once the three Ds + C are removed.

STEP 2: Identify five to eight of the strongest, youngest stems, leaving them tied into the wall or fence. Carefully work your way through the rest of the plant, removing the old gnarled wood in sections down to the ground.

STEP 3: Put your safety goggles on and untie the five to eight healthy stems that are still attached to the wall or fence. They will spring around a bit, hence the goggles. Rewire the wall or fence if necessary with strained horizontal wires at 30cm intervals or individual nails.

STEP 4: Reattach the stems to the wire on the wall or fence in a fan pattern, ensuring each stem is as horizontal as possible. Cut all sideshoots from the main stems back to a few buds. These two processes will guarantee flowers in summer.

STEP 5: As with any radical prune, the plant in question will need a nutrient boost to help it regenerate. Roses are especially hungry, so go for a combination of fish, blood and bone along with a hefty mulch of manure.

THE DIFFERENCE BETWEEN CLIMBING AND RAMBLING ROSES

Climbing and rambling roses look pretty similar to the casual observer but the way they grow and therefore how they need to be pruned is very different. As I mentioned earlier in this chapter, climbing roses produce flowers on wood they have made in the current season and are pruned accordingly (see left). Rambling roses are different in that they flower on wood produced during the previous season. What this means in terms of pruning and rejuvenation is that ramblers need pruning directly after flowering in summer. This way they will produce new stems before the year is out that will go on to flower the following year.

Other plants that can be treated this way

For climbing hydrangeas and clematis see pages 81 and 87 respectively. Other climbers, such as *Jasminum officinale*, *Vitus*, *Passiflora* and *Trachelospermum* can be treated in a similar fashion to the climbing rose, focusing on producing a stripped, back, structural framework.

STEP 6: Pay off! Four months after restructuring and rejuvenating a climbing rose it will have produced flowering spurs from the horizontal stems and bare areas at the base of the plant will be clothed thanks to repositioning the stems.

Spring-flowering shrubs

Spring-flowering shrubs are among the bulkiest in the garden, and left unmanaged they quickly become overgrown and reduce their flowering. Rejuvenating these plants can be approached in two ways. The radical but risky approach simply involves felling the whole plant to some 10cm from the ground. It carries several risks, not least that this sort of prune may kill an aged shrub or trigger the emergence of weak sappy growths that never really form a shrubby structure. But it can often spark a tired woody specimen back to life. The safer strategy is a staggered revival similar to the subsequent spring prunes the shrub will require in future. If you opt for the full-fell option, this is best carried out in early spring, so that when the plant's sap rises it will be directed to dormant buds in the stumps, triggering them into growth. Alternatively, the stagger revival is ideally carried out just after flowering in late spring or early summer.

PRUNING FOR STAGGERED REVIVAL

STEP 1: Assess the overall form of the shrub. Ideally you'll be aiming to create a well-balanced symmetrical plant, so start by removing any wayward branches right down to the ground using a handsaw. The branches are often tightly packed, so be sure to avoid damaging nearby stems as you cut.

STEP 2: Next, remove around one-third to half of the oldest branches all the way to the base. Many of these older branches will be supporting the younger ones that have emerged through them, so don't be surprised if the shrub becomes a little floppy as you remove the old wood.

STEP 3: You should now be left with a series of one- and two-year-old stems, and little else. Initially some of these young stems will be weak and may need supporting but don't stake the plant in the long term as movement in these stems is what will thicken and straighten them up. Feed after pruning as per roses (see page 68).

STEP 4: Repeat the process in two years' time to complete the revival.

Other shrubs that can be treated this way

Abelia, Clerodendrum, Corylus, Deutzia, Dipelta, *Euonymus europaeus*, Exochorda, Forsythia, Leycesteria, Philadelphus, Ribes, Rubus, *Viburnum x bodnantense*

Wisteria

Not only are wisteria extremely beautiful, with their grape-like inflorescences, but they are also among the longest-lived plants in the garden. Single specimens can easily make it to well over 100 years old and can become almost tree-like with their heavy basal trunks supporting vast expanses of flower-laden stems. Left to their own devices their rampancy can see them turn into truly huge, weighty plants, but this mighty scale is often out of kilter with most gardens. Bringing them back into check depends on how old the plant is. A specimen up to 20 years old can be rejuvenated with relative ease, while those of 50–100 years plus are more of a challenge.

REJUVENATING WISTERIA WITH TRUNKS UP TO 5CM IN DIAMETER

STEP 1: A relatively young wisteria that is out of control can be brought back to good productivity with a hard prune in late winter. Identify all the whippy stems from the previous year and cut them back to about 30cm.

STEP 2: With the whippy growth removed you should now be able to see the main structural stems of the climber. These stems do have some flex so can be repositioned to fill gaps on the wall or fence if necessary.

Use strong twine to tie in, rather than wire.

STEP 3: Aim to splay out the structural stems in a flat fan, tying-in growth as horizontally as possible and bearing in mind their relative position from one another and how long the flowers of each stem will trail.

STEP 4: To encourage flowering, cut all sideshoots (potential flowering spurs) down to four or six buds. The climber should now focus its energies on these buds, turning them into spring flowers. Getting it wrong is no disaster, though, the worst that will happen is you'll miss a year of flowering.

Well-pruned wisteria will drip with blossoms in late spring.

Rejuvenating wisteria with trunks up to 15cm in diameter

Plants of this scale are relatively manageable, if a little woody. To revive them, remove a few of the heaviest trunks, getting rid of any tangled masses in the process. Then prune any sideshoots emerging from the main stems back to three or four buds.

Rejuvenating wisteria with trunks more than 15cm in diameter

It is possible to revive ancient plants if their flowering has slowed or they are simply too big. Radical as it sounds, trunks up to 30cm in diameter can be felled to within 20cm of the ground in spring, effectively reducing the whole plant to a stump. The wisteria will quickly generate fresh whippy stems from the base that need tying-in. The process may see the plant without flowers for a few seasons.

Apple trees

Glorious old apple trees are a common sight in established gardens. More often than not a succession of owners will have attempted various prunes over the years, leading to oddly shaped or poorly fruiting trees. However, with the correct rejuvenative pruning, over a few years, it is possible to hold on to the aged glory of an ancient apple while turning it back into a productive tree. The bulk of this work is best carried out in winter when the tree is dormant.

REJUVENATING A POORLY PRUNED APPLE

STEP 1 (Year 1) Assess the tree for health, looking out for canker and other diseases. If these are present and significant then it may not be worth retaining the tree. Better to replace it with a healthy new cultivar nearby but not on the exact same spot as the existing apple tree.

STEP 2 (Year 1) Remove any dead, diseased or damaged wood, bearing in mind that removing much more than one-quarter of the timber from the tree will potentially trigger a mass of new, unproductive water shoots. To alleviate congestion in the tree and form a goblet structure to the crown, aim to remove one or two substantial central trunks back into the crown. You may find shoots emerging near these prunes the summer after the work has taken place – remove them as they appear.

Year 1

Years 2, 3 and 4

STEP 3 (Year 2) Having left the tree alone since the previous winter it is time to begin the second phase of pruning. Trees that have previously been over-pruned will likely have a mass of vertical water shoots. Remove around 50 per cent of these back to the main structural branches and tip prune (10cm) the tops of the remaining vertical stems.

STEP 4 (Year 3) Repeat the work of the previous winter and reduce the number of water shoots by another 50 per cent, carefully pruning back to structural branches. This phased reduction helps reduce the reoccurrence of unproductive water shoots.

STEP 5 (Year 3) The remaining water shoots should have now produced some side branches. Prune back both the tip of the water shoot and its first side branch by around 10cm. This will ultimately help to trigger fruit production. Feed the tree at the base with fish, blood and bone each year after you've pruned.

STEP 6 (Year 4) The tree should now be in a productive state and you can begin a regular annual cycle of pruning to keep productivity high. Apple pruning is a specialist but learnable skill that you can develop over several years once you've established exactly which apple you have. This mystery can be unlocked at Apple Day events around Europe where specialists can identify varieties from apples brought in by gardeners.

Other plants that can be treated this way

Crab apple, pear and quince trees can also be treated in this way if necessary to return them to productivity. However, certain species should not be pruned in winter as this radically increases their chance of fungal infection. Top fruit (stone fruit) trees that should be pruned in summer include cherries, plums, apricots and peaches.

Hydrangea

For blousy colour from mid-summer to autumn, hydrangeas can't be beat. The most commonly cultivated forms are the mophead macrophylla types whose rejuvenative pruning is addressed in the step-by-step instructions here. There are, however, other types of hydrangea with different revival pruning requirements.

Hydrangea paniculata are grown for their large conical flower spikes and need a hard prune every year whether you are in the process of revival or not. The whole shrub can be cut back to near ground level, just above the lowest pair of active buds in spring before leaf-break. The popular *Hydrangea arborescens* 'Annabelle' should be treated in the same way.

Hydrangea quercifolia, *H. aspera* and *H. villosa* are grown as much for their attractive foliage as for their flowers. Other than the three Ds + C (see page 63) they should never need pruning. If they are aged or collapsed, simply replace them rather than trying a rejuvenative prune.

Lastly, the climbing form of this popular shrub, *Hydrangea anomala* subsp. *petiolaris*, can be revived with a hard cut back to its structural frame in spring but will skip one year's flowering as a result, which is unavoidable.

REJUVENATING HYDRANGEA MACROPHYLLA

STEP 1: Begin the prune in spring before the leaves have emerged. Start by assessing the plant and then removing dead, diseased, damaged and crossing stems in the usual way (see page 63). Scratch through the bark if you are unsure if a stem is alive – those that are alive will be green and a little wet under the bark.

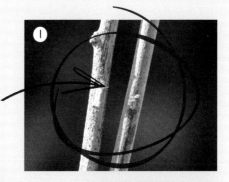

STEP 2: Next, remove all the old dried flowers from the previous season. (Leaving them on over winter not only looks attractive but also provides some protection to newly emerging buds.) Cut the flowering stems down to the first set of fat buds, which will go on to produce foliage and flower this year.

STEP 3: To revive aged and poorly performing hydrangeas you'll need to remove some of their oldest wood. This is easily identifiable as the thickest and most gnarly stems. Cut out between three and five of the oldest stems, down to the ground, ensuring you don't compromise the overall silhouette in the process.

STEP 4: Feed well after the prune with the usual fish, blood and bone or an ericaceous feed to support regeneration and flowering. The addition of sequestered iron at this stage will see pink-flowered forms turn blue over a few seasons.

Euphorbia and basal subshrubs

Euphorbias are a large group of plants with different requirements when it comes to rejuvenation. The herbaceous species that die back to the ground each winter can simply be split and divided in spring if they are becoming tired. More robust evergreen species, such as *Euphorbia characias*, can have dead stems and flowers removed in summer. However, in my experience they do not rejuvenate well from a hard cut back, so they should be replaced if ailing.

The really stocky euphorbias, such as *E. stygiana* and *E. mellifera*, can be rejuvenated with radical cut-backs. Both tend to form a shrubby structure that eventually results in a splay of bare stems with a dome of foliage on top. This can look good for a few years but starts to tire with flower numbers and sizes diminishing. Fortunately these shrubby euphorbias do half the work for you, as they will naturally start regenerating from the base, sending out fresh new stems from ground level before you've even considered pruning them.

Other plants that can be treated this way

A number of shrubby species, such as *Choisya ternata* and hardy fuchsias, behave in the same way as the woody euphorbias. As their top growth starts to slow or peak they begin generating new stems from ground level. Pruning out all the old wood from these plants in spring will focus energy on the juvenile stems at the base, triggering them into vigorous growth and ultimately flowering.

STEP 1: Wear gloves for this job as euphorbia sap is poisonous. Start in mid-spring by assessing if the plant has reached the stage where it is regenerating from the base. If this is the case it's ripe for revival.

STEP 2: Cut the oldest branches back to the base of the plant using either a handsaw or loppers. The stems will be quite hefty so take the weight out first before making the final cut at the base (see page 67). The newly emerging stems will be very delicate and snappy at this stage, so take great care when cutting near them.

STEP 3: With the prune done, dress the soil around the plant with fish, blood and bone, then mulch well.

PAY OFF! This is the rejuvenation, three months after picture 3 was taken.

Evergreen shrubs

Small-leaved evergreen shrubs are essential to the garden in winter for their form and colour and in summer for their bulky contrast to perennials and freer shrubs. Most of them are amenable enough to being topiarised or trimmed into forms to suit your garden. Alternatively, they can be clipped in an organic way so they appear to be free form but are within your control. Most evergreen shrubs are tough enough that they can take a reshaping rejuvenative prune, which will alleviate them of half or more of their foliage and stems, without batting an eyelid. This means that a wild and woolly Pittosporum can be pruned down into a smart ball, or a wayward shrubby Lonicera can be organically pruned to be smaller and revived, but natural-looking.

SHAPING, TOPARISING AND REJUVENATING EVERGREEN SHRUBS

STEP 1: Assess the overall form of the shrub and the way it is naturally trying to grow. Can you work with this form and refine it or does the plant require a total reshape? Will it work best as a piece of topiary or in a freer but managed form?

STEP 2: With a shape in mind, begin pruning in spring using shears. Don't worry about cutting exactly above a bud – these plants will forgive you. Slowly clip away, stepping back from the plant regularly to assess its shape.

STEP 3: Now the shape is loosely defined, finish it off and smooth out its lines using small shears or secateurs. Once the shape is complete, feed with fish, blood and bone. This feed is especially important if you are removing substantial amounts of foliage.

Other plants that can be treated this way

Buxus, small-leaved Cotoneaster, Escallonia, Euonymus, small-leaved Hebe, *Ilex crenata*, Ligustrum, *Lonicera nitida*, *Lonicera pileata*, Osmanthus, Phillyrea, Pittosporum, Teucrium.

Radical revival pruning

Many plants require specific and delicate pruning to gently ease them towards revival, however, there are a huge number of shrubs that need no such coaxing. This is perhaps the reason why they have endured as popular garden plants for generations. The box right lists just some of the garden shrubs that will respond with vigorous new growth and life as a result of a radical 90 per cent prune. The Sambucus pictured in the step-by-step sequence is typical of these sorts of plants that will bounce back from a harsh hack.

Use the technique employed on the Sambucus for any of the plants listed right in spring. They will quickly respond with new growth but be prepared, with at least some of them, to sacrifice flowers during the first season following your cut back. Those that will flower in the same year as you cut them back include buddleja, phlomis and *Salvia microphylla,* therefore you can repeat hard hacks in subsequent years to keep them to the size and shape you need.

Plants that can be revived with a radical 30cm prune

Atriplex, Aucuba, Brachyglottis, Buddleja, *Camellia japonica,* Catalapa, Chimonanthus, *Choisya ternata,* Cornus, Corylus, Cotinus, *Erica arborea,* hardy Fuchsia, Hebe, *Hypericum calycinum,* Ilex, Indigofera, many Kerria, *Prunus laurocerasus, Laurus nobilis,* Lavatera, Leycesteria, shrubby Lonicera, Mahonia, Nerium, Olearia, Osmanthus, Perovskia, Phlomis, Photinia, Phygelius, Pittosporum, bush and shrub roses, Salix, *Salvia microphylla,* Sambucus, Santolina, Sarcococca, *Spiraea japonica,* Syringa, Taxus, Ulex, *Viburnum tinus,* Weigela.

Many plants can be 'hard-pruned' to trigger a substantial rejuvenation.

STEP 1: Take the weight out of the shrub by removing all branches down to 1m or less (see page 67).

STEP 2: Identify dormant or emerging buds and cut just above these some 30cm from the ground.

STEP 3: Feed with a high-nitrogen fertiliser and keep the plant well watered to support new growth.

PLANTS WITH PARTICULAR REQUIREMENTS

Lots of plants in the revival garden can be grouped into broad categories and pruned and rejuvenated following the same principles. There are, however, a number of species with more specific requirements. Pruning them in the wrong way or at the wrong time could spell disaster.

Cordyline and Yucca

These single or multi-trunked woody plants can reach 3m or more. Routine maintenance is little more than removing their dead leaves with no pruning required. However, if the plant is too big it can be cut to 2m, 1m or even 50cm in spring and there is a good chance it will send forth growth from dormant buds hidden under the bark. There is, however, a risk of killing off the plant altogether.

Bamboo

Short groundcovering bamboos can be cropped over and will regenerate fresh foliage and canes with ease but large forms are not so amenable. Cut the stem of, say, a Phyllostachys in half and it will result in the plant producing a fuzz of useless growth on top of the cut cane. Better to chose a bamboo that will climax at the height you want or reduce its footprint by digging chunks away from the base. The whole clump can also be thinned with judicious removals at ground level.

Conifers

Though most ornamental conifers can take a clipping to their outer twigs or be lightly shaped, they won't respond well to a radical prune. The bulk of these plants will simply die if you cut back into the old wood. If they are just too large, consider replacing them with conifers that can be clipped, cut, reshaped and topiarised, such as Taxus or Thuja. For more information see page 184.

Clematis

These beautiful climbing plants are split into three groups. Those that flower early in the season, such as *C. montana,* are in Group 1. They, along with the summer-flowering Group-2 forms, can usually take a radical hack back to structural stems in spring, but they will skip a year's flowers as a result. The late-flowering Group-3 clematis should never present a problem, though, as their cyclical prune is down to 20cm from the ground every year in late winter.

Phormium

I've seen some truly horrifying attempts at pruning phormiums over the years. The simple message is don't do it! The chopped-off tops of leaf blades will simply remain as they are cut, resulting in a mutilated plant. If a phormium is too big, consider replacing it. There are cultivars ranging from 50cm to 3m tall, so there is sure to be one to suit your space. All it will ever need is the removal of dead leaves from the base.

Lavender

Occasionally an aged lavender can be rejuvenated from a hard cut back, but in most instances pruning into old wood will kill the plant. Lavenders are often cited as being short-lived, but with a light prune after flowering they can be maintained in good form for a decade or more. Once the flowers have faded, remove them and their stems, reducing the overall foliage silhouette by no more than 5–7cm.

Hedges: evergreen and deciduous

The green walls created by hedges are fundamental to screening, dividing and protecting gardens. But over time they can degrade, leading to bare patches, excessive width or height and gaps at the bottom. Hedges can also become much wider at the top than the base, which can cause them to collapse in heavy snow or rain. All of these issues can be rectified but it will take longer to reap dividends than with other forms of rejuvenative pruning. There are several stages, taking between three and four years to complete, but once done it's possible to maintain the refreshed 'green wall' to the height and width you want – forever!

A shabby, holey hedge can be rejuvenated back to good health with timely pruning.

Hedges that will rejuvenate from hard cut backs

Aucuba, Carpinus, Crataegus, Elaeagnus, Fagus, Griselinia, Ilex, Ligustrum, Photinia, *Prunus laurocerasus*, Taxus, Thuja.

... and those that won't

Chamaecyparis lawsoniana,
× *Cuprocyparis leylandii*.

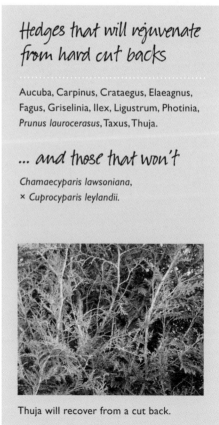

Thuja will recover from a cut back.

REJUVENATING HEDGES

STEP 1: (Year 1) Start in late winter to spring with the sunniest side of the hedge first to ensure the results of your pruning will grow away as quickly as possible. Identify the main trunk and cut all stems on your side of the hedge back to within 10–15cm of the main vertical trunk. Then cut the other side of the hedge as usual, leaving the bulk of its growth uncut. Feed as per roses (see page 70).

STEP 2: (Year 2) Allow a year to pass and the side you cut back hard will have sent out fresh new growths. These should not be trimmed but left to fill out for the year. If growth is substantial, consider cutting back the other side of the hedge in the same way as the sunny side. If it has not recovered much yet, give it another year.

STEP 3: (Year 3) By year three both sides of the hedge should have now been cut back virtually to the main trunk and will have produced a lot of new growth. If you did not cut back the top during any of the previous stages do this now, but to around 20cm lower than you finally want it to be. This way it will produce a thicket of growth leading to a dense hedge-top.

STEP 4: (Subsequent years) To avoid the hedge degrading in future, be sure to carry out annual prunes from late summer onwards. Always aim to make the hedge wider at the bottom than at the top. This not only looks better but also prevents splitting and allows the maximum light to strike all the way down to the hedge's base.

PLANTS TO LEAVE ALONE

There are several species of garden plant that simply don't respond well to pruning. They are either unable to regenerate from old wood and die following a hard cut back or pruning them triggers the emergence of sappy, weak, fast-growing and vertical 'water shoots'. These unprunable plants are best left to their own devices and only pruned to remove dead, diseased or damaged wood.

Species that don't respond well to most forms of pruning include: Araucaria, Banksia, Carpenteria, Chamaecyparis, Corylopsis, Daphne, Paeonia (tree peony), Picea, Rhododendron, Thymus, *Viburnum plicatum* 'Mariesii'.

Magnolias do not respond well to regular prunes.

eradicate & reinvigorate

A garden revival is a fine balance between what you decide to keep, improve or remove. Weeds need eradicating early on in the process, once you've identified them, and then, both turf and – most vitally – soil are likely to need reinvigoration. These three tasks are the next major works to tackle after you've carried out initial analysis and pruning.

Remove weeds

Identifying what is a weed and what is a cultivated plant is one of the first challenges when reviving a garden. Pages 26–9 will help you figure out what to remove and what to retain, but then comes the next challenge: how to eradicate the weeds without damaging the plants you want to keep. Techniques vary from easy hoeing off, through to sustained applications of weedkiller. Some weeds will succumb with ease, while others will battle it out for months or even years. Thankfully these resilient weeds don't tend to make up the bulk of the problem for most gardens.

Weeds can be broken into several distinct categories, and over the years I've devised simple strategies to eradicate them.

GERMINATING ANNUALS: *Euphorbia peplus*, bitter cress, chickweed and groundsel

Hoeing is the simplest way of managing annual weeds. Pick a hot sunny day and hoe the weeds off at root level, leaving them on the soil surface to dry out and die. If the annual weeds you are tackling are going to seed then don't hoe them off as this will simply spread the seeds. Instead, hand-pull them and burn or throw them in a container of water to rot down over several months. The resulting 'soup' won't win any Michelin stars but it can be applied to the garden as a gentle food.

Aim to hoe through the garden every few weeks as some of the most efficient annuals, such as hairy bitter cress, can go from seed to flower in as little as six weeks. Knocking these weeds back at every attempted resurgence will eventually reduce the 'seedbank' and therefore the amount of germinating weeds.

There is much truth in the old gardening adage: 'one year's seed is seven years' weed', so keep up the good work and it will, eventually, pay off.

1. Pernicious bitter cress can grow and flower near year-round.
2. Many brassica relatives are prolific garden weeds.
3. *Geranium robertianum* is a common but easily removed weed.
4. Creeping buttercup is amoung the most difficult weeds to eradicate.

ROOT-CREEPING PERENNIALS:
ground elder, mare's tail, couch grass and buttercup

These plucky plants won't give up the ghost without a fight – and a protracted one at that! They are the weeds that have haunted gardens I've managed all over the world. Often, after much effort, they'll seem to disappear, only to return a year later with even greater vigour. But don't let this put you off. You will, as I have, win eventually.

Start by weakening the plant by digging out every scrap of root you can muster. Most of them will regrow from fragments little more than a centimetre long, so diligence is key. These plants will reappear pretty quickly so be prepared to do the same again, forking through the soil to remove fragments. With the plant weakened, at least a little, it is time to set to with chemicals. I'm no fan of this approach but some weeds are simply unmanageable without toxic intervention. The challenge in applying chemicals is avoiding them affecting surrounding plants.

The most effective herbicide for tackling these nasties is glyphosate. It works by translocation so is absorbed by the leaves and then travels through the plant's vascular system, killing it in two to three weeks. Unfortunately, it will also have the same effect on any ornamental plant it comes into contact with. To mitigate the potentially negative impact on your plants, garden wildlife and the wider environment, there are a few easy approaches to adopt. First, always spray on wind-free days in the early morning or just before dusk when insects are least active. Secondly, don't spray on a sunny day as much of the herbicide will evaporate. And finally, protect your plants by applying herbicide to the weed leaves with a wipe, to avoid spray drift. (Alternatively, you can protect surrounding plants with plastic to prevent them getting splashed.)

You will see the top growth wither within a few weeks of applying the herbicide. Unfortunately, just like in a good horror movie, the bad guys will return when you least expect them, so be prepared to treat them another one or two times to ensure 100 per cent annihilation.

TAPROOTED PERENNIALS: dandelion, thistle and dock

Thanks to a lengthy and determined taproot these perennial weeds can hang around for years robbing ornamental plants of light, water and nutrients. Removing them involves extracting every last millimetre of the taproot. This can be done by digging around the weed with a spade, lifting out a clod of soil with the taproot contained and then breaking away the soil to reveal and remove the whole beastie – taproot and all.

A translocated herbicide such as glyphosate can also work. It is best applied as a weed wipe, rather than a spray, to avoid drift. It can with one or more treatments eradicate these taprooted terrors!

CLIMBERS: bindweed and *Bryonia dioica* (bryony)

Climbing weeds are all but impossible to treat while they are wrapping themselves around other plants. Start by removing all the foliage and stems, marking the place the plants emerges from the soil with a long bamboo cane. In a matter of weeks the plant will have re-emerged and will start climbing the cane. This isolates the climbing weed from other plants, meaning that when it's a metre tall you can apply a translocated herbicide such as glyphosate by means of a weed wipe. This can be enough to kill off the roots, too, but it may need a second application.

Left for a year or more woody weeds such as ash or *Acer pseudoplatanus* can becomes challenging to remove.

SHRUBBY AND TREE WEEDS: Fraxinus, acer, bramble, sambucus, Japanese knotweed and ivy.

Of all the plants to invade our plots it's the woody species that are the most unwelcome. From an initially fragile seedling these woody weeds quickly develop strong roots and an even stronger will to survive. If you catch them in the first year it's usually possible, with some effort and gloved hands, to pull them out yourself. But by year two a spade will be required and by year three a brush cutter and lots of sweat. If you discover any of these woody undesirables on your plot then remove them before they get a real foothold.

Japanese knotweed is unfortunately not so easy to eradicate. It can be dug out but treatment is perhaps best left to specialist firms who use a strong herbicide that they inject into the plant.

KEEPING WEEDS AT BAY

No matter how diligent your initial weed eradication, it is a sad fact that they will return. This is due to either the 'seedbank' of weeds in the soil that comes to the surface each time you cultivate, remaining root fragments that can spark back to life or distribution by animals or the wind.

Paved surfaces and gravel are easy to manage ongoingly and organically by 'scrubbing out' emerging weeds with a block-paving wire brush or by using a weed burner. Managing weeds in beds is more complicated. Ideally you'll fill the garden so full with beautiful ornamentals that they'll smother any emerging weeds, but in reality there will always be bare bits of soil where seed will germinate. To mitigate this the simple solution is mulch. A loose material, such as garden compost, composted green waste, milled manure or bark chips, works well through herbaceous plantings. It also has the benefit of retaining moisture and adding nutrition. For shrub plantings it's possible to up the ante by using a geotexture, a permeable landscape fabric, on the soil surface before smothering it with loose mulch. This 'belt and braces' approach works for shrub and tree plantings but not for spreading clumps of perennials, which will eventually lift the fabric as their stems spread underneath it.

Other than these approaches it is simply a case of observation and diligence. A dock takes seconds to hoe out as a germinating weed but 10 minutes to dig out if it gets established, so the trick is to stay ahead of the game.

Revive the soil

Soil is the lifeblood of any garden and perhaps the most significant factor in bringing it back to good health. Without a flourishing soil rich in organisms, organic matter and nutrients, all other efforts will be in vain. A plot that has not been tended to could have numerous problems lurking beneath the surface. Pages 29–31 deal with how to assess your soil and its condition. Here I suggest some near-universal remedies that can redress problems ranging from poor drainage and compaction to bad structure or nutrient depletion. I'll also highlight the different forms of organic matter, supplements and mulches suited to different soil problems.

REMEDIES FOR SOIL PROBLEMS

It is not as difficult as you might think to make radical improvements to a poor-quality soil. It's all about adding the right stuff and letting nature do the rest.

Compacted soil
Fork over the soil to at least 35cm, or deeper if a profile pit (see page 30) has indicated a deep compaction pan. Add organic matter in the form of well-rotted farmyard manure by double digging. If it is a clay soil, consider adding lime to reduce stickiness and the reoccurrence of compaction.

Dusty, light soil
Double-dig organic matter into the soil in open areas and mulch heavily annually with bulky organic matter, such as farmyard manure. For planted areas, simply add a heavy mulch annually. Some people use water-retaining crystals on dry soil to increase its water-holding capacity.

Isolated, poorly drained soil
First ascertain if the soil type or its structure is to blame. A profile pit (see page 30) will reveal compaction or iron pans along with the underlying soil type. Depending on their depth, these can be broken by single or double digging, which will aid drainage. If the drainage issue is caused by clay soil then organic matter and/or lime will help.

Sharply drained soil
Dig or double-dig organic matter into the soil in the form of manure or compost. This will aid water and nutrient retention and encourage plants to root widely, thus stabilising the soil. Add feeding supplements to counter nutrient loss and mycorrhizal fungi, too.

Nutrient-depleted soil
Add organic matter to the surface (mulch) and sub-surface and dress areas with supplements, such as bone meal, fish, blood and bone or chicken manure. This will both aid retention of nutrients in the soil and hugely boost what is currently lacking. Add mycorrhizal fungi, too.

Poorly structured soil
Work organic matter deep into the soil with 40cm+ trenches when double digging (if topsoil depth allows). Kept well mulched, soil organisms will work bulky matter into the earth and improve its structure.

Capped silty soil
Break the capping with a good fork over followed by digging organic matter into the first 30cm of soil (single digging) and mulching heavily to reduce the impact of rain, which can cause capping.

DOUBLE DIGGING

This age-old practice has revived gardens, beds and borders for generations.
It is a useful technique for unplanted areas of soil that require reinvigoration.

STEP 1: Dig a trench 30cm wide and deep across the width of the area.

STEP 2: Move soil from this trench to the opposite end of the area you are working on.

STEP 3: Fill the trench to 15cm deep with manure and dig it in.

STEP 4: Dig a second trench next to the initial one, using its spoil to fill the first one.

STEP 5: Dig manure into the bottom of the second trench and continue the process.

STEP 6: Use the soil from the first trench to fill the final one. Job done!

Composted garden
waste and/or manure
can breath life
back into tired,
depleted soils.

ORGANIC MATTER TO IMPROVE SOIL

Farmyard manure

Source and buy manure from local farms or garden centres. Ensure the manure is 'rested' and not still steaming hot and active. Delivery is often by the trailer load but can also be sourced in tonne bags or 80-litre sacks. As ever, greater volume reduces price. Farmyard manure adds structure, water retention, drainage, nutrients and bulky matter to the soil. Use it for double digging, planting and mulching.

Milled manure

This specialist product is the result of farmyard manure being milled into chunks smaller than a golf ball and part-composted. It is sometimes available bagged in garden centres but more commonly from compost specialists who will deliver it loose or in tonne bags. It adds everything farmyard manure brings to the soil but probably releases nutrients quicker. Use as per manure. It is especially good as a self-binding mulch.

Composted green waste

In many areas the local authority composts garden waste and the resulting compost is available to purchase bagged. Composted green waste usually has a reasonably fine texture though its nutrient levels will vary widely depending on its source materials. It can also be delivered in bulk and will improve the soil structure, add to its bulky matter and increase nutrients, but not to the same level as manure. Use as per manure.

Garden compost

If you are lucky enough to have an existing compost bin then make the most of its contents. Otherwise, consider setting one up in a quiet corner of the garden as a future source of food and mulch. Garden compost has reasonable nutrient levels but can vary wildly so should not be relied upon. Use it for planting, mulching and double digging.

Peat-free compost

Made from a combination of different materials depending on the brand, most peat-free composts consist of composted bark, composted wood waste, green waste and other recycled materials. The product is, of course, environmentally friendly and can be purchased bagged or in bulk. It is often quite light in texture and nutrient levels vary between brands. Use it for planting, mulching and double digging.

SUPPLEMENTS TO IMPROVE SOIL

Lime
Made from ground limestone, garden lime is sold in most garden centres and nurseries. It has two specific uses. One is to raise the pH of the soil, the other is to flocculate clay soil. This medieval-sounding practice is nothing more than the lime being applied to clay to bind its particles, which improves structure and drainage.

Bonemeal
Unsurprisingly this ground bone product is derived from abattoir waste. It works well as an autumn or spring fertiliser as it boosts root production and is relatively slow release when scattered on the soil's surface or dug in. It can be purchased bagged from garden centres and should be stored in a cool, dry place. Apply bonemeal by gloved hand at the recommended rate.

Fish, blood and bone
Fish, blood and bone is a ground-down version of its eponymous title. The three components provide nitrogen, phosphate and potassium to the soil. It can be either scattered on the soil's surface or lightly forked in at the start of the season. Buy it bagged at the garden centre and store it in a cool dry place. Use it according to the manufacturers' dose rate noted on the bag and wear gloves.

Mycorrhizal fungi
Although relied on for years by the nursery industry, the validity of mycorrhizal fungi has been called into question of late. It is a powder containing specialised fungi that live symbiotically with plant roots and expand their nutrient- and water-grabbing web.

I have found mycorrhizal fungi successful in rectifying the problems associated with planting a new rose on the site of an old one, so it can work.

Chicken manure
This pelleted product is literally what it says on the tin. It is high in nitrogen so can be used as a spring boost for most plants but err on the side of caution as it is quite rich. Buy it from garden centres in bags or drums and apply it with gloved hands to a forked soil surface. A word to the wise: it can be a bit stinky when it first goes down.

Comfrey 'soup'
Strictly a homemade product, this 'soup' is simply made by rotting down the leaves of comfrey in an old bucket or water butt. The resulting fluid, after a few weeks of brewing, is rich in phosphate and can be used virtually anywhere in the garden as a liquid feed. *Symphytum officinale* (comfrey) is easy to grow in a spare corner of the garden and can be harvested several times a season.

Mulches to improve soil

Bark chips
Produced as a byproduct of the timber industry, bark chips are available in various sizes from 5mm to 5cm. They have low nutritional value but work effectively as an attractive, weed-supressing mulch on borders. Buy them from garden centres in bags or for a greatly reduced rate loose or in tonne bags. I always avoid products supplemented with wood chips as they are less than attractive.

Grass clippings
Mowings from the garden are a useful resource. They can be used in compost heaps, in fine layers, to keep the compost hot, wet and active. Mowings can also be used as a mulch. Employed this way they deliver low-level nutrients to the soil but bind together well to retain moisture and supress weed growth. Think twice about using grass clippings if your lawn is full of weeds as it could spread their seeds.

Mushroom compost
Available from specialist suppliers and occasionally garden centres, mushroom compost is waste material from mushroom growing comprising mainly compost horse manure. Its nutrient levels vary and it is usually quite alkaline, which can alter the soil pH levels it is dug into or added to the top of as a mulch. It is easy to handle and makes for a smart border surface. Buy it in bulk from local specialists.

Composted straw
This increasingly popular product, the result of composting shredded straw, is sold bagged at garden centres and in bulk from specialist suppliers. Use it as a mulch across beds and borders where it will bind well on the surface helping with water retention and weed suppression. Nutrient levels are not high but it does eventually work into the soil, increasing organic matter.

Revive turf

Bringing a lawn back to life is one of the most gratifying jobs when you're reviving a garden. Unlike pruning or soil improvements you can get results fast. In a matter of weeks it's possible to turn a lawn from lacklustre to lovely. I'm not the biggest fan of lawns but they do serve a purpose in many gardens, providing paths, seating areas, play areas and from an aesthetic point of view, the connective tissue that pulls the whole plot together. You may decide to scrap the lawn altogether, in which case there is advice on alternative lawn plants on page 105. If you are looking to retain and improve the lawn, turn to page 101 for how to assess its problems and find appropriate resolutions.

Reinvigorating your lawn is relatively easy and usually inexpensive. With an investment of time and the right remedies you can rectify the problems that unloved lawns suffer and turn them back into luscious carpets of green.

Turf tips

Past revival? If your turf has turned into a lanky feral meadow, no amount of tinkering will bring it back. Instead, opt for a radical strim and rake-off followed by removing the turf with a hired turf cutter, then prepare the soil for new seed or turves.

Thin and patchy

The underlying cause of thin and patchy turf can often be the soil it is growing on. Before reseeding or trying to address the problem on the surface, have a dig around in the difficult patch. Page 31 gives advice on the condition of soil and directs you to advice on how to redress it.

The problem of patchiness often results from one of three factors: not enough drainage, too much drainage or subsoil that has been brought to the surface and won't support ordinary plant growth. Subsoil is generally paler than topsoil and can be removed, replaced and reseeded. Problems associated with too much or not enough drainage are tackled on page 96. Once the soil is sorted, it's time to reseed or turf the patchy area (see page 105 for how to do this).

Shaded

Most grass species are evolved to grow in full sunlight, so if an area of lawn has become shaded many of the species that make up the sward (mix of grasses) die out. There are two approaches to redress this problem. One option is to create a bed in the shaded area and plant it up with shade-tolerant species. Option two is to resow the area with a grass species that can cope with shade. Garden centres and online retailers sell shade-mix grass as seed and a few companies supply turves for shade. How to lay turf or sow seed is covered on page 105.

Broad-leaved weeds

A neglected lawn is often a weedy one. Broad-leaved weed species, especially those with low-growing habits, manage to skulk below the mower blade and evade removal. The weeds that typically do this include dandelion, plantain, selfheal, buttercup, daisies and clover. The taprooted species among them, such as dandelion, can be removed by hand with a knife to get rid of shoots and roots but others are more of a challenge. Unfortunately, unless you are prepared to live with a weedy lawn there is only one option – herbicide. These are available in the form of selective weed killers specifically for lawns. They come as either liquid or granules and only target the non-grass species. It may take a few treatments to remove the most stubborn weeds but with ongoing maintenance you should rarely need to treat again. If you end up with bare patches as a result of weed removal, reseed or returf the area (see page 105).

Disease

There are many diseases of grass but thankfully most of them only tend to occur significantly on overmanaged turf, such as golf greens. Most are forms of fungi that can be treated by specialist fungicides, available from garden centres or via a turf management specialist. Look out for the following symptoms and treat if necessary: white powdery leaves, rusty marks on leaves, yellow die-out spots, red webbing between the grass blades or white fluffy growths on the leaves. Once rectified, overseed the area (see page 105).

Pests

Lawn critters can wreak havoc on turf left unchecked. The worst tend to be chaffer grubs, leather jackets and moles. The first two pests are evident on turf when birds start pecking at specific areas in an attempt to eat the turf-root-munching grubs. An investigation of the area will reveal holes and loose and dead turf. These two pests can be managed by applying nematodes (microscopic worms), which will kill the grubs, or by laying old carpet or black plastic across the affected areas to encourage the grubs to come to the surface of the turf overnight so they can be brushed off and destroyed.

Moles are not so controllable. In my experience the problem is best left to a local mole catcher, but a gardening friend swears by removing the innards of musical birthday cards and sealing them in a bag placed in the mole's hole. After hearing 'Happy Birthday' for the thousandth time I might be tempted to leave, too.

If large areas of lawn have died out as a result of any pest then overseed (see page 105).

Moss

Although it can feel lovely underfoot, moss in the lawn will weaken and even kill off the grass. It can be removed by a rake or scarifier (see left). Alternatively, a moss killer, available from garden centres, can be applied across the lawn. It will take a while to show any effect but the moss will eventually turn black and die. Moss is often a symptom of poor drainage so it is worth considering improving the drainage under the lawn. Overseed affected areas (see page 105).

Thatch

The build-up of dead leaves, debris and cut grass that accumulates in turf is known as thatch. It needs removing annually or it can lead to diseases. The simplest method is raking it out but a scarifier can be hired to remove it. This piece of kit looks like a lawn mower but is designed to extract thatch, which once removed can be added to the compost heap. Scarifying also has the added benefit of removing moss. Overseed any areas left bare by thatch removal (see page 105).

The build-up of dead grass, moss, weeds and debris can compromise a lawn if left unchecked.

REVIVE YOUR GARDEN

HOW TO LAY AND PATCH LAWNS

Overseeding

Bare areas of turf can be brought back to life with overseeding. The process is straightforward. Where there is a reasonable amount of grass already, simply scatter seed across the surface and keep well watered. Where the grass is much thinner, prepare the soil by removing weeds, thatch and dead grass. Spike the soil with a fork to 10cm deep, creating a fine crumb structure. Gently compress this. Or, if the bare patch is tiny or already has up to 50 per cent sward coverage, simply rake the soil surface open. Scatter seed over the area ensuring it spills over into the surrounding turf. Rake the seed in lightly and, as an extra measure, crumble a fine layer of soil (less than 5mm) over the sown area. Keep it well watered and it will (between spring and autumn) germinate within a few weeks.

Seeding new or damaged areas

Seeding a new lawn follows the same process as above, except it is worth taking extra time to level the whole area with a rake. Once the soil is lightly dug (spiked) it will also appreciate a quick shuffle over with your boots to compress it, followed by a second light rake over. Scatter the seed by hand following the supplier's recommended rate. The easiest way to assess this is to weigh out the recommended per-metre dose and scatter this across a square metre of paving. This will show you how dense the seed should be on the ground in order to be at the right rate. Once the seed is down, rake over the area again and then keep it damp for the first few weeks as it begins to germinate. After six to seven weeks you'll be able to make your first tentative cut, but avoid walking on the lawn before then.

Laying turf

Before starting to lay turf, it is important to get the soil right. Once you've addressed any problems with the underlying earth (see page 31), remove any existing turves using a turf cutter, which can be hired locally. These turves can be stacked upside down in a corner of the garden where they will slowly

break down to form useful loam. Next, turn over the area to be turfed with a fork to around 15cm deep, removing roots, weeds and debris in the process. Tread the soil down again and use a wide rake to break it into fine crumbs and level it out.

Turf can be ordered by the square metre from local suppliers. Pick a rye grass mix if the turf is likely to get a lot of wear or a mix higher in bent grass if it's more ornamental. Turves will arrive rolled and can be left that way for up to 48 hours before they start to degrade. Keep them damp and in the shade.

Start laying the turf in rows across the garden, beginning at the back of the house. It may seem odd but the established technique is to lay a row and then work on top of that row (with scaffold boards) to lay the next row. Aim to lay the turves in a brick pattern ensuring their edges meet on all sides. Use an old kitchen knife to cut any challenging shapes such as around beds.

It's a fast process, once the prep is done. Keep the new turf well watered and within a month or so you'll be able to enjoy the fruits of your labours.

Alternative 'lawns'

Neat lawns are not everyone's style and in small gardens they can be more trouble than they are worth, but there are a few no-mow alternatives. Chamomile and thyme form dense green mats that will take a small amount of walking on. They are best established as small or plug plants. The camomile to use is a non-flowering cultivar called *Chamaemelum nobile* 'Treneague', while in terms of thyme I'd opt for the red creeping form *Thymus serpyllum* 'Coccineus'. A newer alternative to turf lawns is micro clover. This mini version of clover can be walked on at the same frequency as grass, barely needs cutting and is very drought tolerant. Find seed suppliers online and sow as per lawn grass.

shape up

Reviving a garden presents a great opportunity to reassess its design and alter it to suit your needs; however, the process of redesigning an established plot is quite different from starting with a blank canvas. Your initial assessments and revival operations will have established what you want to keep and it's these elements – be they trees, shrubs or bits of hard landscape – that present the challenge. They need to be incorporated into the design in a manner that neither compromises them, nor the overall layout. But before thinking about how the garden will look and feel, take a few steps back and have a think about how you want it to function.

Key functions of your garden

As the great modernist architect Le Corbusier once said, 'Form follows function'. In other words, your starting point should be based on the key functions your space needs to perform. To formulate and understand these, it's useful to make a scale sketch of your garden. Pace or measure it using a scale of 1:50 or 1:25. On a drawing with a scale of 1:50, 2cm will represent 1m in reality; on a drawing with a scale of 1:25, 4cm will represent 1m. Choose whichever scale suits your garden and the size of paper you have, but don't get too hung up on exacting precision at this stage.

The next step is to indicate functions and routes. Think about pleasure and practicality and ask yourself the following questions:

- Which are the sunniest bits of the plot that might be suitable for a seating area?

- What is the most sensible route from the house to any outbuildings, summerhouse or glasshouse?

- Do you need open turf for kids to play on or for you to sunbathe on?

- What is the most sensible route around the garden?

- Where will the washing line go and how will you get to it on muddy winter days?

- Which are the main areas you can see from the house during winter and summer?

- Do you have enough storage?

- Where should the compost bins go and how do you get to them?

- Which views out of the garden do you want to retain or enhance?

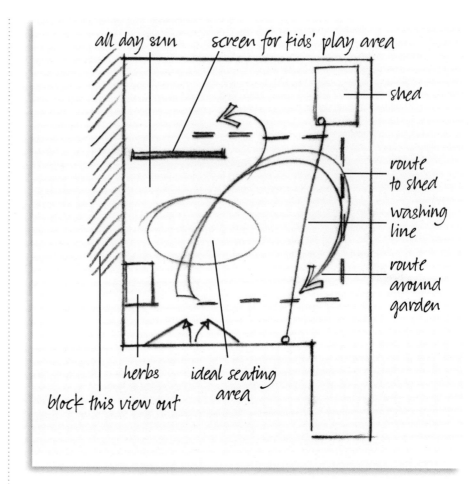

- Which views out of the garden do you want to disguise or block?

- Do you want to grow veg and if so where is it best placed?

- Do you want to grow herbs and can these be planted close to the kitchen?

- Do you need to break the garden into separate spaces for different functions, say: play area, veg plot, wild garden, formal borders, seating areas, etc?

- What does your initial analysis of the garden tell you in terms of opportunities and constraints?

As you ask yourself each of these questions and sketch onto the plan potential resolutions. Mark out areas with their different functions and the routes between them, and take into account the elements of hard landscape and trees/shrubs you've chosen to retain, though don't try to absolutely resolve a design at this stage. You should wind up with a sketch similar to the one shown above. This is your 'form follows function' (FFF) sketch.

Garden styles

With the basic functions of the garden established it's time to think about the style of the space and its physical layout. There is such a rich gardening heritage that there is no shortage of styles to emulate, and choosing an overall feel will help with your garden's cohesion and unity. Styles to consider adopting or altering to your own purposes include: cottage, Japanese, tropical, New Wave European, formal English, contemporary, Mediterranean and Arts and Crafts.

COTTAGE

The spirit or essence of a cottage garden is abundance. However, the very first gardens of this kind were, in truth, predominantly vegetable plots attached to cottages in feudal villages where workers would grow food to supplement their meagre income and diet. Through a shared fantasy developed over the last few hundred years, we've somehow landed at the idea that these little gardens are all about hollyhocks, roses and more floriferous perennials than you can shake a stick at. Though this palette of plants may not be true to the origins of cottage gardens, they are beautiful none the less. To get the look go for cutesy wooden arches with scented vines, meandering paths flanked with roses, herbaceous plants and lots of glorious self-seeders. Throw in the occasional millstone, birdbath and picket fence and the fantasy is beautifully fulfilled.

TROPICAL

A garden composed purely of species from the tropics will not survive the European climate but it is possible to create the spirit of 'tropical' with a range of hardy tropical-looking species and plants that can be shipped outdoors come spring and returned to a warm refuge in autumn. Somewhat like cottage gardens, quasi-tropical ones in Europe have developed a shorthand style that calls for large and texturally contrasting leaves and hot colours such as reds, oranges and yellows with a few clashes thrown in for good measure. Of course, gardens or landscapes in the tropics don't necessarily look like this but somehow, in Europe, we've decided that red flowers and big leaves equals tropical.

JAPANESE

There are at least five distinct styles of Japanese garden, but unless you are a total purist the essence of these styles can be extracted and emulated. I realised after spending time in the country that the spirit of Japanese gardens is essentially a miniaturisation of their natural landscape. Unlike 'traditional English gardens', which contain few native species, Japanese gardens are wholly composed of them. Therefore the essential elements are first and foremost plants, namely acers, cherries, bamboos, pines and sago palms. Secondary, but vital to creating the look outside of Japan, are the hard landscape elements: staggered wooden bridges, tea houses, stone lanterns and flattened puddle stones.

Standing stones, raked gravel and acers all contribute towards a Japanese feel.

Exotic-looking gardens are possible in cooler climes thanks to plants such as the hardy banana Musa basjoo.

NEW WAVE EUROPEAN

The so-called 'New Wave' European planting style first emerged some 25 years ago and has been slowly refined and experimented with ever since. In essence it is about creating natural-looking, predominantly perennial plantings with meadow-like qualities and a selection of species repeated through them. Masters of this field, with their own books explaining how to achieve 'the meadow look', are Piet Oudolf and James Hitchmough. They suggest sets of plants for particular environments in which they will thrive, growing and self-sowing alongside one another.

Repeated perennial plants, along with self-seeders, are essential in creating the 'New Wave' look.

FORMAL ENGLISH

The idea of the formal English garden is in truth an amalgam of concepts drawn from several hundred years of our gardening history. Influences include the great landscape designers Capability Brown and Humphry Repton but also borrow from Victorian, Georgian and Edwardian approaches. In essence the formal English garden has a rectilinear or symmetrically curved layout with clipped and unclipped evergreens for structure, bountiful roses, blocked-together herbaceous plants and mixed shrubberies. Paths are likely to be straight or symmetrically curved, as are hedges and borders, with strong vistas, sculptural objects and water in the form of fountained ponds.

Clipped formality paired with floriferous abundance is the essence of the formal English garden.

Ulta modern gardens tend to focus on bold, clean-line architecture paired with strong textural planting.

CONTEMPORARY

The notion of a modern landscape is inevitably in perpetual flux. That said, the best gardens to have emerged from garden design shows over the last decade are strongly influenced in spirit by modernist or post-modernist architecture and minimalism. Many of them limit their palette of both plants and materials to a bare minimum in order to achieve a sense of calm and serenity. Think clean lines, fine-cut stone paving, steel structures and water in rills or rectilinear pools. Add to that a touch of meadow planting, rusty corten steel and pale colours for the hard landscape and you have the essence of a contemporary garden.

MEDITERRANEAN

Most of us have a sense of Mediterranean gardens thanks to our propensity to head south for our holidays. The spirit of a garden from this region is based on a few basic materials and a fairly limited palette of plants, but placed together they capture the essence of the Med. Terracotta is, of course, important in the form of pots, roof tiles, wall-top tiles, sculpture and paving. Couple it with whitewashed or extravagantly coloured walls and key plants such as bay, rosemary, citrus, lavender and bougainvillea and you are well on your way to creating a garden with a Mediterranean feel.

ARTS AND CRAFTS

Gardens created in this style, from around 1880, include Hidcote and Hestercombe in England. Designed by Lawrence Johnston and Gertrude Jekyll respectively, these two properties embody the Arts and Crafts ideal of using traditional crafts, coupled with roomed gardens and abundant planting held within formal rectilinear beds and borders. Sissinghurst and Great Dixter in Sussex, England, also display many of these characteristics. In essence, to create an Arts and Crafts feel you'll need hedged or walled 'rooms', worked stone, brick and timber structures and planting (often colour themed) that is a rich mix of herbaceous plants, bulbs, annuals and shrubs.

The 'outdoor rooms' of an Arts and Crafts garden create a sense of intimacy.

With just a few key elements it's possible to capture the spirit of the Mediterranean anywhere in the world.

Marrying functionality with style

The trick now is to marry the functional aspects of your garden with the style you are looking to create and then make the layout on the ground proportionate to the space. A tried-and-tested method for getting well-balanced proportions and lines is to start with the property itself. Do its windows, doors and features suggest a grid or proportioning system that could be extended into the garden? In other words, can you draw lines out into the garden based on the width of the doors or windows of the house?

To keep things simple, have a play around with different grids that can be extended from the house into the garden. This grid system gives you a safety net but don't let your creativity be strangled by it. Just because it is a grid does not mean the garden design has to be rectilinear, straight-lined or blocky. Simply lay the grid over your FFF (form follows function) sketch and see how things might fit. You may have established that the back left corner of the garden is the sunniest and suited to a seating area. How does this fit within the grid? Does it have to be square or rectangular or could it have flowing lines? You may know you need a path from the back door to the garden gate but does this have to be a straight line? Could it initially follow the grid out from the house and then take a curvaceous sweep round towards the back gate, which would also define a curved side to the lawn in the process?

Making use of design tricks

The other aspect of the design to consider at this stage is layering in some design tricks. These simple ideas can be injected at almost any point in the design process but are seriously worth considering in order to make the very best of your garden. Like other garden makers, I rely on these 'tools' not only to pull a design together but also to change the sense of space and to inject a particular spirit or unity to the place. Below are suggestions for some tried-and-tested tricks to consider.

ADD RHYTHM AND REPETITION

The reason so many show gardens and professionally designed plots feel cohesive is simply due to the presence of unifying elements. These elements might be trees, bulbs, path surfaces or topiary, but by repeating them through a space it suddenly becomes a rhythmic whole. To enhance the effect further the elements often have a relationship. Maybe rusty-coloured spring tulips pick up the orange-brown colour of corten steel planters or a mass of self-seeded, pale blue nigella at ground level are just a few tones away from the eucalyptus overhead. However you choose to do it, a touch of rhythm and repetition will bring a sense of togetherness to your garden.

SIMPLIFY WITH SYMMETRY

Symmetry has been a guiding principle behind much architecture and garden design for over three thousand years. Creating symmetry in the garden is a cinch and it often naturally occurs as part of the design process: think double borders, archways, pergolas, gateways, pairs of pots and so on. It is genius in its simplicity. Symmetry can even be paired with the idea of rhythm and repetition by repeating double sets of topiary, for example, symmetrically along two double borders.

PLAY WITH SEASONAL AND CHANGING COLOUR

Colour-themed borders can make for beautiful planting schemes, however, they are often one-hit-wonders, peaking with colour for only a matter of weeks in summer. To make garden colour really work you need to think across all the seasons. There is no reason why a mixed planting can't have a predominantly pastel scheme of pale blues and yellows in spring, followed by a summer of pink and mauve herbaceous plants, and be completed in autumn with shrubby species that take on great leaf colour. All three of these components can be achieved in a space little bigger than a few square metres if you choose the right plants. Following the example above, it could be: *Nonea lutea*, *Myosotis* and peach tulips for the spring shift, through which emerges allium, phlox and campanula, backed by *Euonymus alatus* for autumn foliage. Then throw in an evergreen for winter colour and that's all the seasons sorted. The key message is to think through and plan what every bed and border will be doing in each season.

WORK WITH FORM AND VOID TO 'SCULPT' THE SPACE

It might feel like an abstract notion if you are not accustomed to thinking in this way but in essence your garden is a series of forms and voids. In other words, a set of solid objects with gaps between them. These gaps and solids are the bedrock of a garden – they form its structure and architecture. The solids set up 'frames' that provide views and vistas through the space (the voids).

The exciting aspect when contemplating this idea in a garden is that the forms and voids alter through the seasons as plants grow, change shape or lose their leaves in winter. Another factor to consider is linking together the voids in beds where, for example, you've removed many plants but left a few key structural species. To pull these back together as one will take a series of 'void'-filling plants.

A well-divided garden often feels substantially bigger than it really is.

USE DIVISION TO 'ENLARGE' THE SPACE

Breaking up a garden with divisions is one of the easiest ways to enhance its sense of space. A long narrow garden, say 4 x 16m, will feel utterly different if it is broken into four 4 x 4m rooms (with hedges). The feeling of space is enhanced further still if the entrances and exits to each 'room' are diagonally opposite one another, causing you to walk in a zig-zag down the garden. The approach needn't negate long vistas either. By cutting 'windows' through the hedges or plantings it's possible to frame the longest view in the garden, too.

A glimpe into a new landscape is sure to draw the viewer in to explore.

VISUAL TRICKS TO CHANGE YOUR PERCEPTION

Changing the sense of space in a garden is surprisingly easy. Trompe l'oeil is a historic style of painted murals, often employed on walls and buildings. These paintings are designed to trick the eye by creating a false sense of perspective and depth. Similar effects can be achieved by using mirrors in the garden but these can present a risk to birds, who fly into them.

'False perspectives' can also be achieved using hard landscape and plants. If a path is designed to narrow slightly as it moves away from you it will generate a sense of further depth and length. The same trick can be applied if a shrub or tree is repeated through a space but each specimen gets closer to the previous one as it gets further away from the viewer.

Perhaps the easiest trick of the lot is the Japanese idea of borrowed landscape (shakkei). By framing trees and features outside your garden with the trees and features contained within it, it is possible to 'draw in' bits of the surrounding landscape to make them your own.

AN APPROACH TO PLANTING DESIGN

Your revived trees, shrubs and plants, coupled with the functionality you need and the style you are adopting, will drive your planting design process. There is no absolute format to it, but if you stick to a few basic rules (and break them occasionally) you'll be en route to creating a garden that brings you joy 365 days of the year.

- In mixed borders aim for around one-third evergreen plants to provide winter structure.

- Don't just choose 'green' evergreens, pick those with blue, gold, burgundy and silver foliage.

- Choose several long-flowering species and repeat, repeat, repeat through the beds for unity.

- Unify plantings by repeating topiary in the same shape, say cube or ball, through them.

- Ensure early interest with bulbs and speedy woodland species.

- Ensure late interest with several plants that display strong autumn colour.

- Use grasses or bamboos for movement and sound.

- Sow self-seeders – they will form a seedbank in the soil and germinate if a gap opens up.

- Green tones will form the bulk of any planting, so aim for contrast in hues and textures.

- Slot in some near-perpetual-flowering plants such as erysimum or *Rosa* 'Bengal Crimson'.

- Consider a few pot or field-grown mature specimens to bring instant change to the garden.

- Provide food for wildlife with seed- and fruit-producing species.

- Use bulbs for colour bursts, such as alliums for late spring and *Gladiolus murielae* for autumn.

- Consider layering clematis or annual climbers over existing shrubs for added interest.

- Plants don't need to be grouped in odd numbers, use them in twos or sixes if you wish.

- Ensure contrasting floral forms in herbaceous plantings. Think spikes paired with umbels.

- Consider an overriding colour theme in foliage and flowers.

CASE STUDIES: Ripe for revival

Every garden is different, from its soil and light levels to its character, relative rainfall and existing plants, so there is not a one-size-fits-all option when it comes to design. However, each of the following case studies has a series of challenges common to many gardens:

1. Victorian Terrace Garden

2. Modern City Courtyard Garden

3. Semi-detached Garden

4. Detached Garden

The resolutions for these plots can be applied, extended or shrunk to fit numerous spaces.

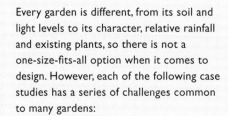

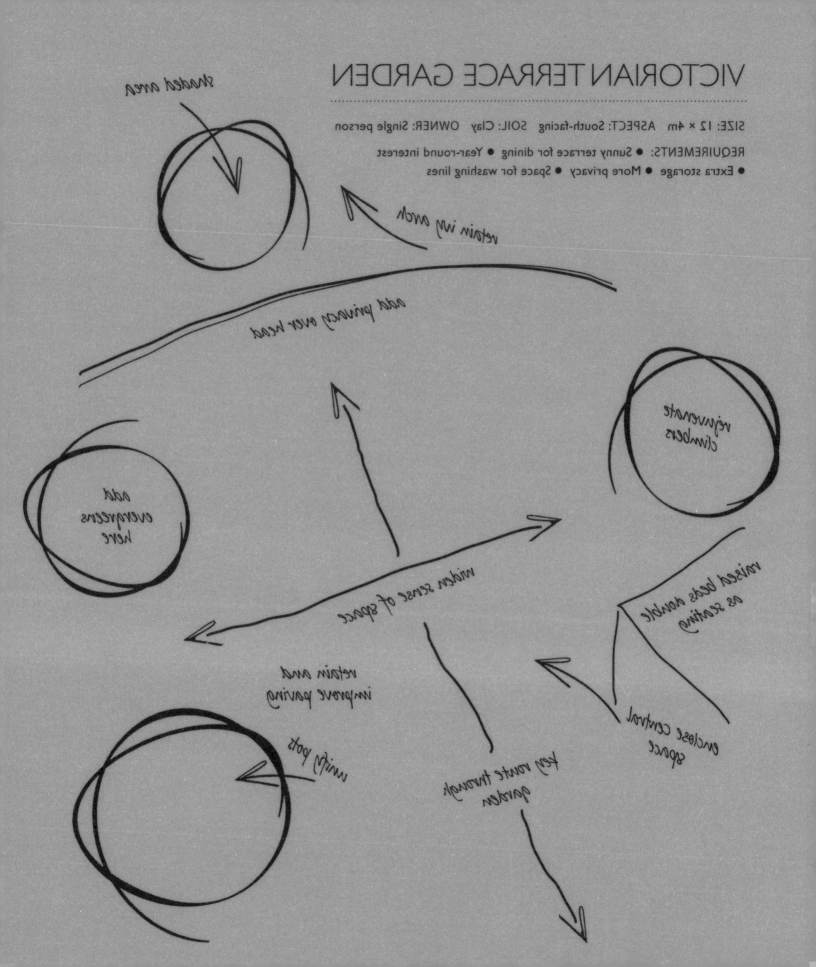

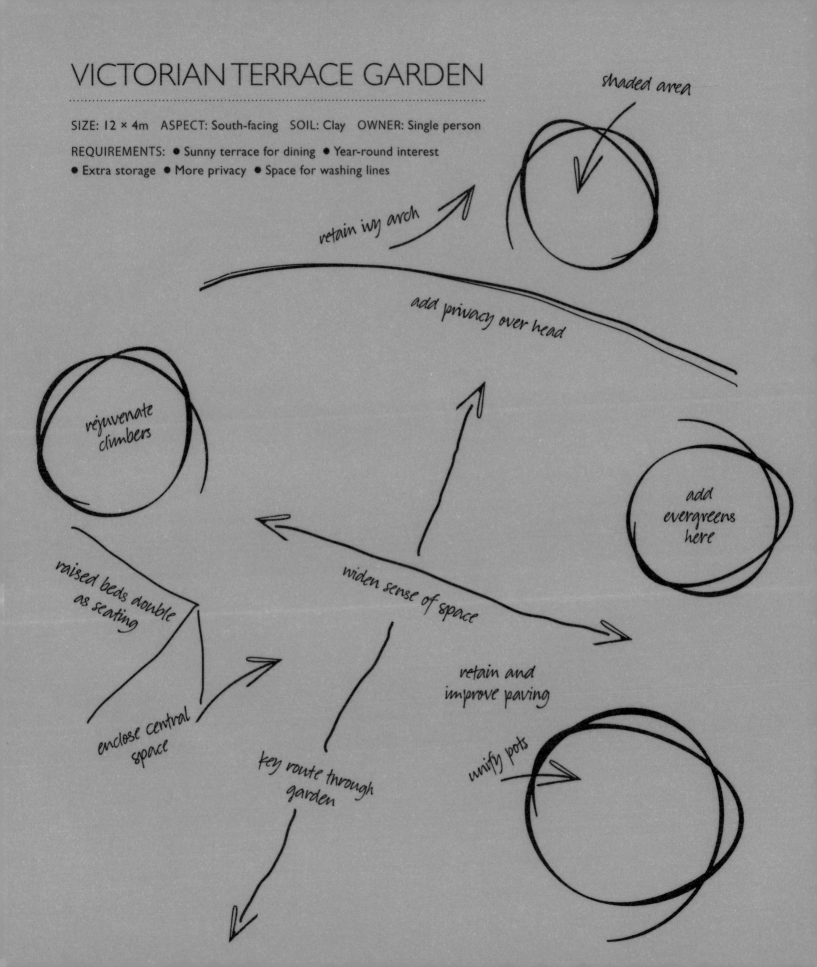

VICTORIAN TERRACE GARDEN

SIZE: 12 × 4m   ASPECT: South-facing   SOIL: Clay   OWNER: Single person

REQUIREMENTS: ● Sunny terrace for dining   ● Year-round interest
● Extra storage   ● More privacy   ● Space for washing lines

shaded area

retain ivy arch

add privacy over head

rejuvenate climbers

add evergreens here

raised beds double as seating

widen sense of space

enclose central space

retain and improve paving

key route through garden

unify pots

MODERN CITY COURTYARD GARDEN

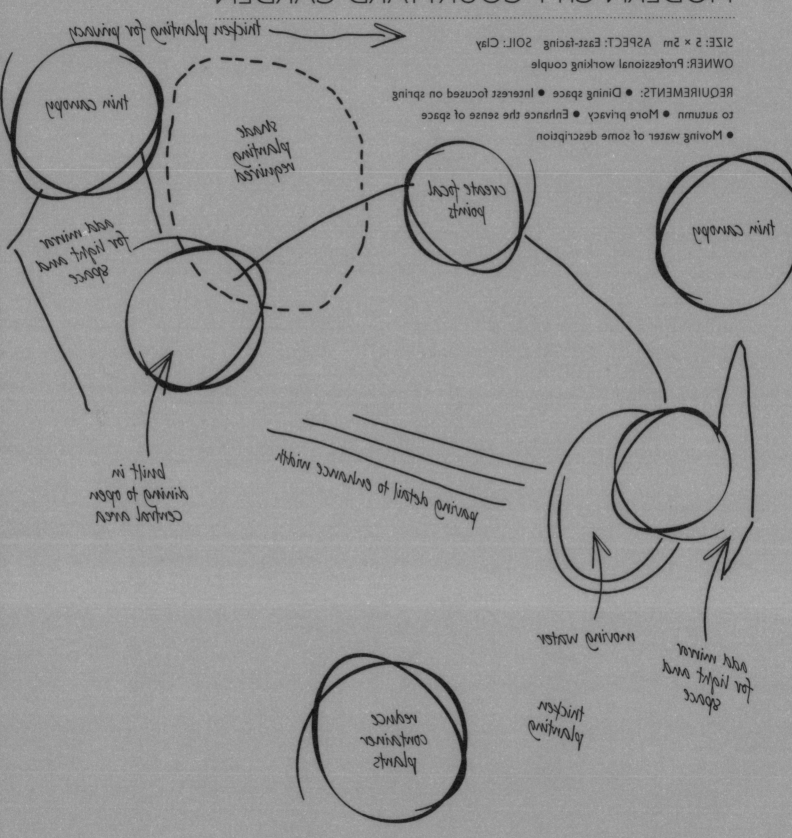

MODERN CITY COURTYARD GARDEN

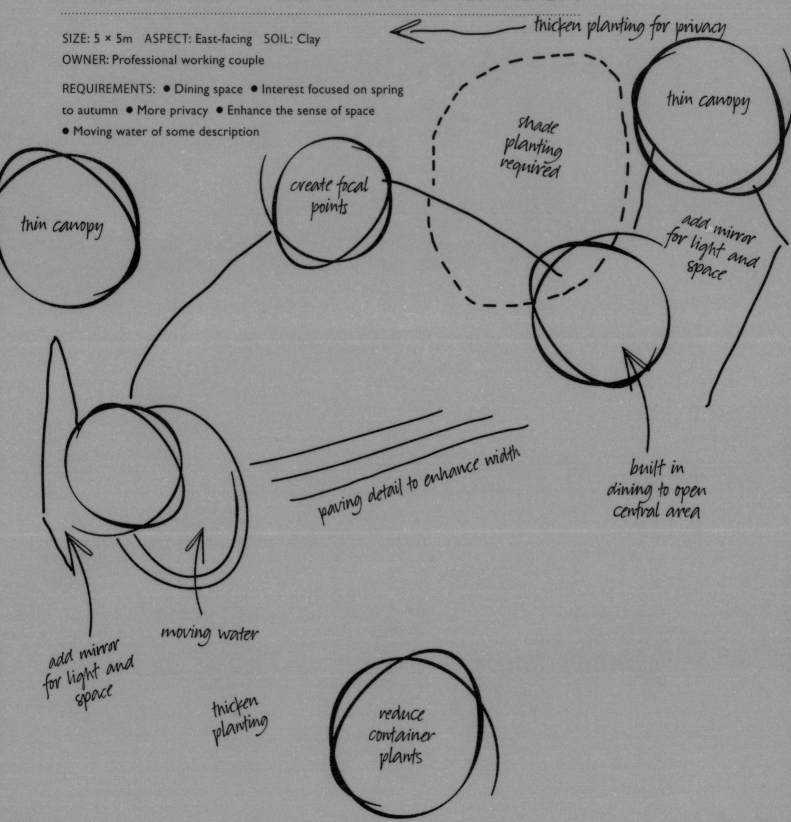

SIZE: 5 × 5m   ASPECT: East-facing   SOIL: Clay

OWNER: Professional working couple

REQUIREMENTS: ● Dining space ● Interest focused on spring to autumn ● More privacy ● Enhance the sense of space ● Moving water of some description

thicken planting for privacy

thin canopy

create focal points

shade planting required

thin canopy

add mirror for light and space

built in dining to open central area

paving detail to enhance width

add mirror for light and space

moving water

thicken planting

reduce container plants

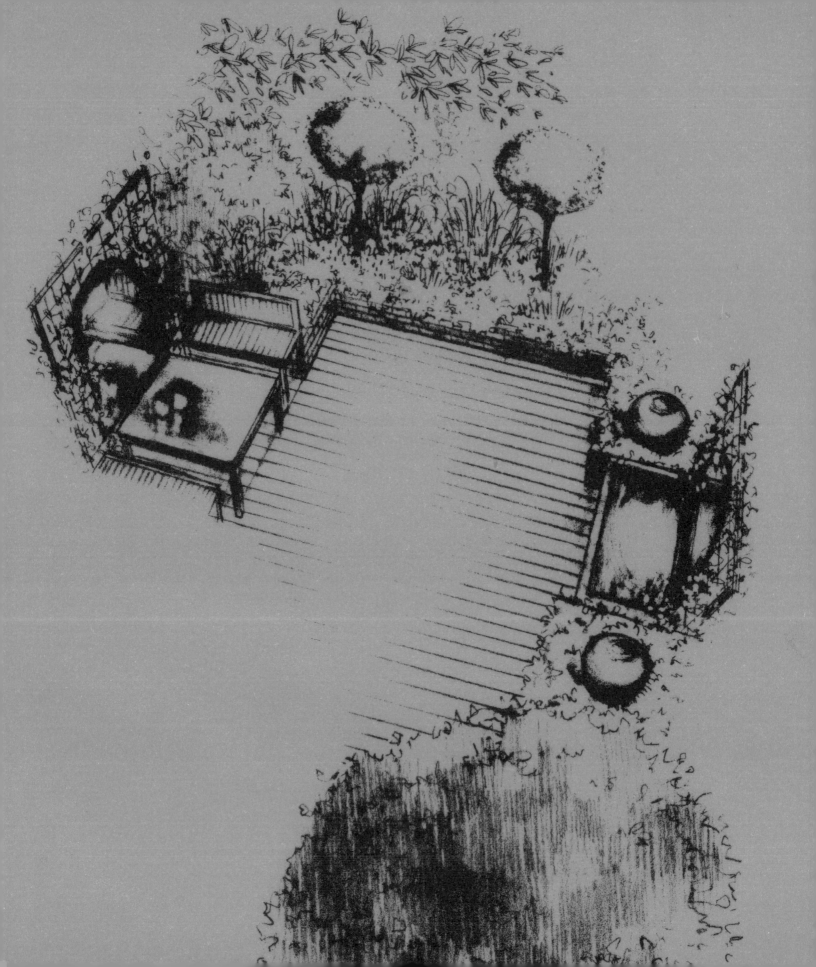

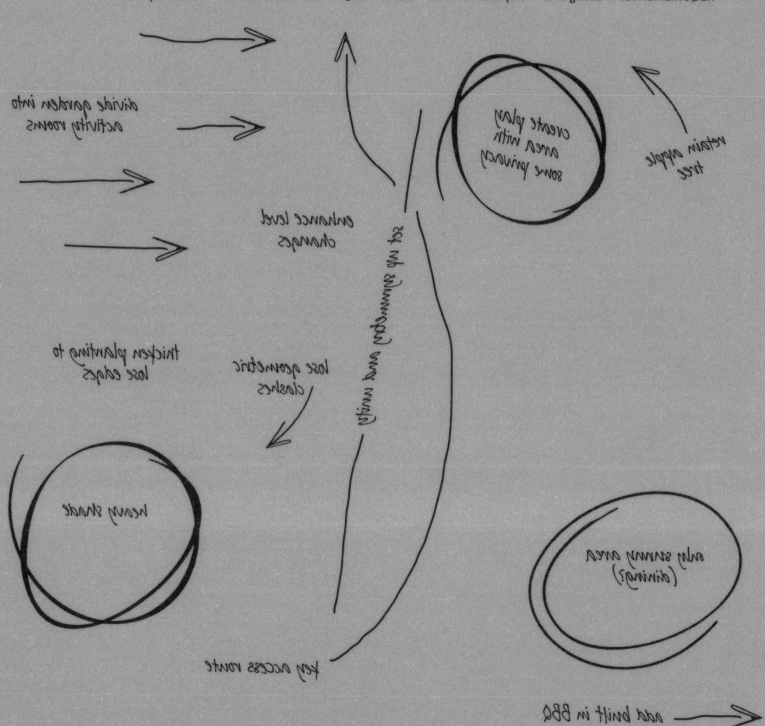

SEMI-DETACHED GARDEN

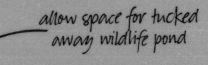

allow space for tucked away wildlife pond

SIZE: 7 × 18m   ASPECT: North-facing   SOIL: Silty clay   OWNER: Young family with two children

REQUIREMENTS: ● Eating area ● Play area for kids ● Built in BBQ ● Year-round interest ● Wildlife pond

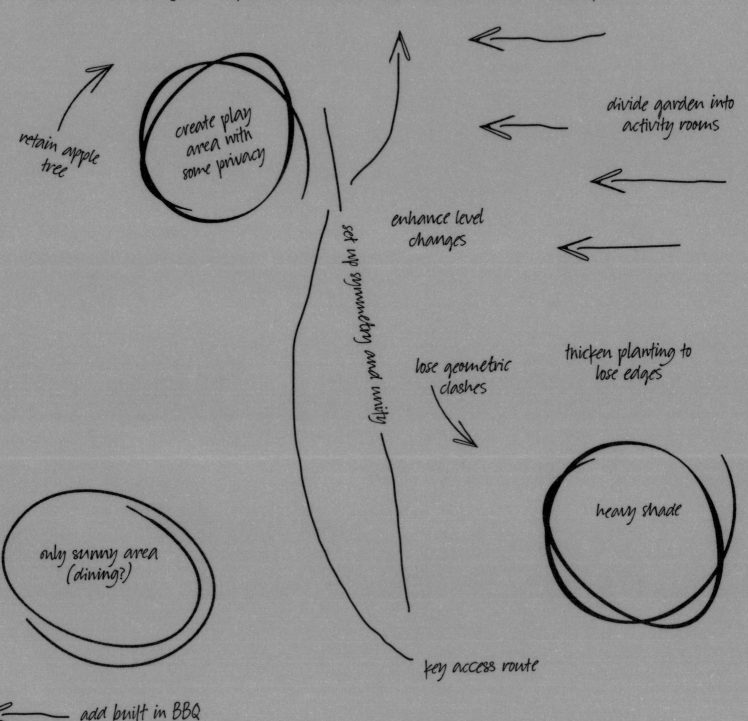

retain apple tree

create play area with some privacy

divide garden into activity rooms

enhance level changes

set up symmetry and unity

lose geometric clashes

thicken planting to lose edges

heavy shade

only sunny area (dining?)

key access route

add built in BBQ

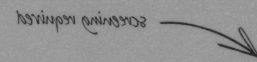

DETACHED GARDEN

SIZE: 20 x 40m   ASPECT: South east   SOIL: Sandy loam   OWNER: Retired couple - passionate gardeners

REQUIREMENTS: • Divide up the space • Soft lines • More planting space • Garden terrace for dining • Veg plot

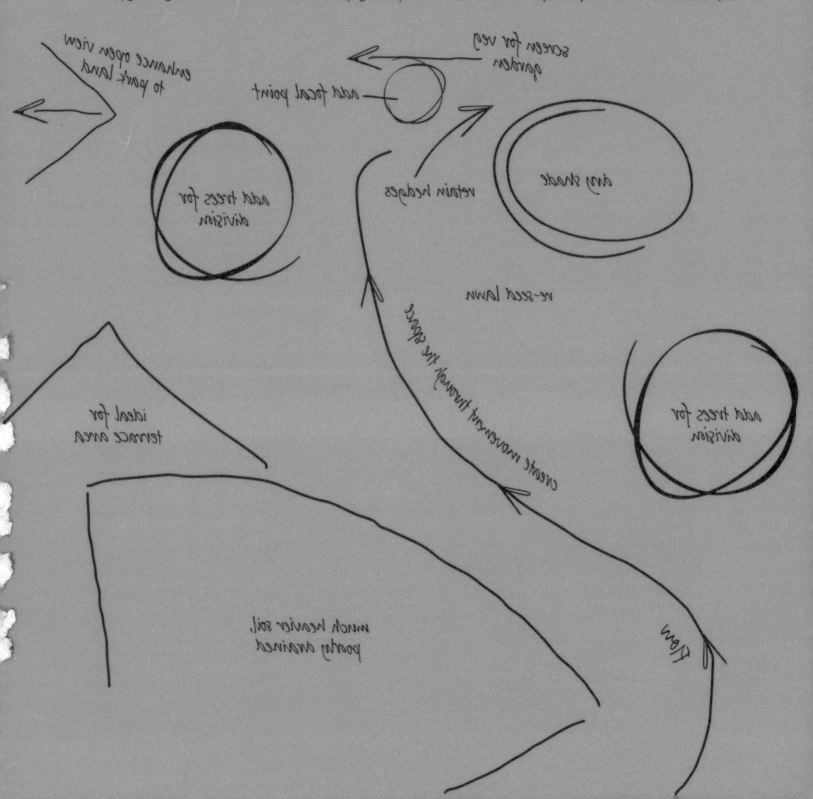

DETACHED GARDEN

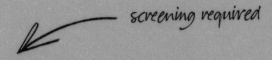

screening required

SIZE: 20 x 40m   ASPECT: South east   SOIL: Sandy loam   OWNER: Retired couple - passionate gardeners

REQUIREMENTS: ● Divide up the space ● Soft lines ● More planting space ● Garden terrace for dining ● Veg plot

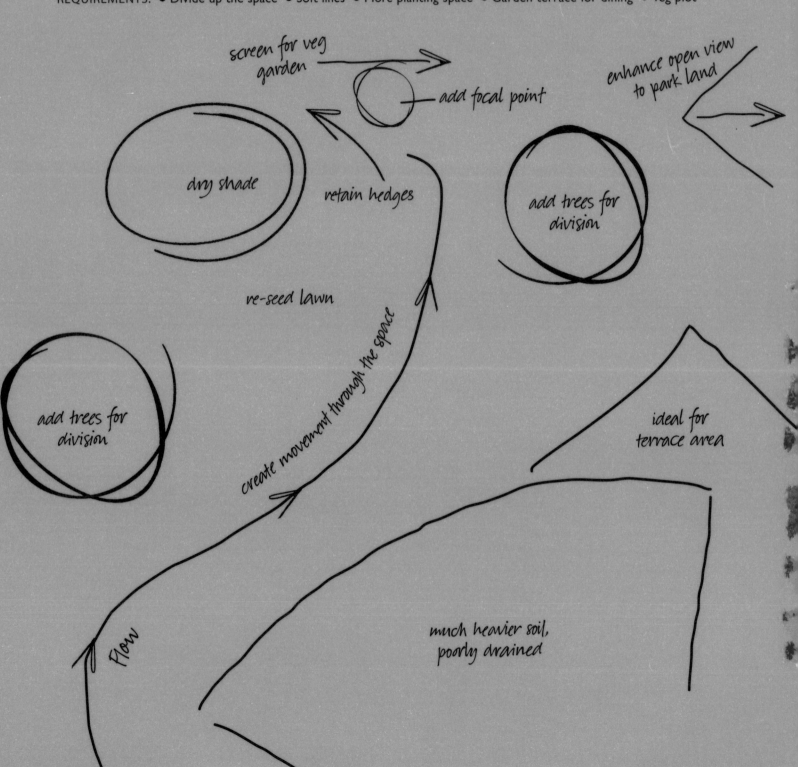

screen for veg garden

add focal point

enhance open view to park land

dry shade

retain hedges

add trees for division

re-seed lawn

create movement through the space

add trees for division

ideal for terrace area

Flow

much heavier soil, poorly drained

edit & move

Once you've understood your garden's foibles, then comes the editing stage. Essentially, this is all about making the most of what the garden already has to offer in terms of its existing plants. Some will be in the right spot already, others may need moving, while some simply need propagating to make more of them. The edit process takes in everything from annual and herbaceous plants to bulbs and aquatic species.

Moving shrubs

It's possible to move surprisingly large shrubs and conifers as long as you pick the right season. The dormant period from late autumn through to early spring is the ideal window for moving both deciduous and evergreen shrubs and conifers as their sap levels will be low and growth activity all but stalled. Over the years I've got away with moving various large specimens up to 2m tall, but this is only possible with the right preparation and aftercare.

If you are planning on moving a large shrub then ideally you'd cut a ring about 50cm around its base with a spade the year before. This way the shrub will produce lots of fibrous roots on the end of the cut tips, thus allowing it to absorb water faster when it is moved. That, of course, is an ideal scenario. If you don't have the time to wait a year then make a start in the depths of winter, so long as the soil is not frozen. If it is possible to prune the shrub in question to reduce its stems by 30 per cent or more,

this has the benefit of reducing water loss in spring when it starts to produce new leaves. It also serves to balance the disparity between what is about to be a radically reduced root system and the crown of the plant. Once the pruning is done (see page 133 for how to make use of prunings), it's time to start digging. Aim to create a trench some 30cm wide and 50cm deep circling the shrub. And go for a root ball size of around 60–70cm, if possible. Then get the spade into the bottom of the trench and start undercutting. If you are on a sandy soil the 'root ball' will start collapsing at this point, whereas clay will remain a sticky lump. Once the roots are free, rock the shrub to its side and slip a loose-weave hessian sheet as far underneath as you can muster. Then tip the shrub back the other way and drag the hessian underneath the root ball – this may require some assistance. The hessian can then be tightly tied around the root ball and the shrub is ready to be hauled out. A sack barrow is my preferred

transport method and will certainly save your back.

Prepare the new planting pit by digging a hole 50 per cent larger than the root ball of the shrub you've lifted and mixing some quality peat-free compost into the base. Getting the shrub into the hole can be as much of a challenge as getting it out of the original one! Try tipping it off the sack barrow and rolling it. It works and it saves a lot of sweat. Once the shrub is in place and you are sure its 'best face' is facing forwards, slowly backfill soil in 15cm layers, compressing it each time to ensure the shrub is both stable and the new roots will be in contact with their water source. Note, I've not mentioned removing the hessian. This can be left on to preserve the root ball from further damage. The roots will penetrate the hessian in the first few months and two years down the line the material will have rotted way, feeding the shrub in the process.

To ensure water gets direct to the roots of the moved shrub, form a soil moat around its base. This way water will be directed straight down to the roots, thus avoiding run-off. Alternatively, bury 1m of flexible 100mm pipe in the planting pit, leaving just a few centimetres sticking out above soil level to shove the hosepipe in.

If the shrub has a huge crown it may also be worth staking it at this point, especially evergreens, as their year-round foliage means they will be buffered by the wind before they begin to get roots down. Finally, apply a dressing of bonemeal around the base to support root development in spring. To ensure good establishment and prevent transplant shock, keep a close eye on watering for the first year, until the plant is able to look after itself.

Propagating shrubs

One of the side benefits of moving large shrubs and conifers are the prunings you are left with. Many of these can be propagated straight away as hardwood cuttings. This is the easiest form of propagation you'll ever do and, in the dormant season, it literally takes seconds.

Start by selecting a 40cm length of stem, ideally around pencil thickness. Make a cut just under a node on the bottom of the stem and then make an angled cut 40cm above it. This angled cut has two functions: it allows rainwater to run off the cut top and it reminds you which end should wind up pointing skywards. Cut a slit with a spade into some spare ground out of the way and push the cuttings in by around half their length (20cm). That's it. Done. Finito. Finished. Come next winter they can simply be dug out and planted as rooted cuttings.

SHRUBS TO PROPAGATE FROM HARDWOOD CUTTINGS

- Buddleja
- Cornus
- Sambucus
- Salix
- Philadelphus
- Winter-flowering Viburnum
- Ribes
- Forsythia
- Abelia
- Deutzia
- Rosa

Moving and propagating herbaceous perennials and grasses

There are many reasons for splitting, dividing and moving herbaceous perennials. Aged clumps start to die out in the centre after a few years, so taking the actively growing sections from the outer edges of the clump and moving them back to the middle is essential. Some are simply in the wrong place and need moving, while others can be split to generate new plants that can be repeated through a border for continuity, used to expand the existing clump or introduced to other parts of the garden. It's a useful and inexpensive way of bulking up plants. The ideal window to do this is much debated. Some say summer, others autumn. All will work, but from my experience late spring is best. This is because the plants are at their most vigorous and determined to grow, even if they have just been chopped into quarters by an eager gardener.

Start by reducing the top growth. This serves to lessen water loss after the move and allows the plant to bounce back sooner. Some smaller perennials are best lifted from the ground whole and split using two forks back to back to prise the roots apart. A knife can also be used for tougher-rooted plants. For larger perennials or substantial stands of them, use a spade to cut out clumps of the plant. As a rough guide, aim for chunks the width and depth of the spade. On clay and heavier soils these clumps will cling together until they are relocated back into terra firma, but on sandy soils it is a different story. The root balls of perennials lifted out of this type of soil tend to crumble, tearing off roots in the process, so a different approach is required. Before even attempting to lift out a piece of plant, have its new hole pre-dug. Cut the chunk of plant away and lift it out lying flat back on the spade. This way it can be carried on the spade direct to its new

Get new plants for free by splitting herbaceous species.

location without having to be put down or shaken about, which can cause further soil and root loss. This may see a little odd, but I promise it works!

Whichever approach you take, the replant process is the same as for moving shrubs. Dig holes around 50 per cent bigger than the split clumps, add some peat-free compost, firm the plants in well and give them a good soaking. They will freak out and wilt for a few days but with diligent watering they'll soon get a foothold and be self-sufficient within a matter of weeks.

Herbaceous perennials and grasses to split and divide

Aster, Phlox, Solidago, Echinops, Geranium, Centaurea, Stipa, Hosta, Astrantia, Veronicastrum, Miscanthus, Helenium, Leucanthemum, *Lychemachia*, Campanula, Delphinium, Persicaria, Anemone, Carex, Thalictrum.

A substantial geranium such as this one can be divided into six or more individual plants.

How to plant

No matter whether you are planting a 2-m specimen shrub or a tiny alpine species, your process and technique will have a huge impact on how successfully that plant will establish. True, plants are real survivors and will likely struggle on to see another day if they are badly planted. But those same plants given a 'red-carpet' introduction to your plot will establish faster, be more able to take up water, flower better and manage to stand on their own two feet much faster than if they are hastily shoved in. Good planting ensures they are able to penetrate the soil, resist pests and diseases, establish relationships with the organisms around them and break out of any spiralled root pattern they have started to develop in the pot.

Basic considerations and process can be applied to virtually any plant. Firstly, location is key (see page 14), then consider the soil you are planting into. Does it suit the plant you've selected or does the soil need altering in terms of its drainage, nutrients, relative acidity or alkalinity? With these factors established you're ready to start planting.

STEP 1: Start by identifying the 'best face' of the plant with the fullest branching and best structure. This is not so important for annuals and perennials but it is vital for shrubs and trees.

STEP 2: Dig a planting hole around twice the width and depth of the plant's root ball, leaving the excavated and broken-up soil nearby ready for firming in.

STEP 3: Add garden or peat-free compost to the hole and the excavated soil. Aim for at least the same volume of compost as the root ball of the plant. Mix the soil and compost.

Watering

Ensure good establishment with regular watering during the plant's first year in the ground. This is especially important for larger specimens in pots of 10 litres plus.

STEP 4: De-pot the plant and un-spiral the roots of woody species (annuals and perennials can be left alone). Then part-fill the hole with the compost and soil mix, settling the plant in on top.

STEP 5: Use the remaining compost and soil mix to firm the plant in. Ensure good contact between the roots and the new medium and firm in the plant, avoiding pushing on the top of the root ball.

STEP 6: Level off the soil, avoiding burying the plant deeper than it was growing in the pot, and make a small soil ridge around it so water is directed to the roots rather than running off.

Collecting and sowing seeds

Reviving a garden offers many recycling, regenerating and repurposing opportunities. One of the easiest is the collecting and resowing of seeds. This process is a sure-fire way of getting new plants of the species you want, virtually free.

There is no great mystery surrounding seed collection, it is just a question of careful observation. If you spot something in the unrevived garden that you like, want to repeat elsewhere or simply bulk up, then keep a close eye on it. There are no exact timings for collecting seeds as both the seasons and the plant will behave differently each year. The trick is to keep an eye on the plant as soon as it has flowered. Check it every few days and it will tell you when the seed is ready. As they ripen and the pods turn brown and begin to disperse, that is your moment. Gather the seedheads in brown paper bags or similar, being sure to name and date the bags, and place them in a warm dry place to allow the seed to fully dry out. Leave for a few weeks and then shake out the seeds into smaller packets and store them in a box in the fridge until you are ready to sow.

Depending on the type of seed you collect there are a few different ways to sow. If the seed is from a perennial or shrub then sowing is best in a John Innes seed compost in small pots. Compress the compost, thinly scatter seed over the surface, then sieve over a fine layer of compost. A propagator will aid germination, but failing that water the sown pots from underneath and seal in a plastic bag in a warm place that is light but out of direct sunlight. Most spring-sown seeds will appear in a matter of weeks. Once germinated, they can be pricked out or transferred into individual pots to grow on. After four to six months many will be ready to plant out into the garden, though shrubs can take longer to bulk out.

Annuals are a different matter. Tender ones can be treated as above but hardy ones, such as limnanthes, agrostemma and eschscholzia, can be sown direct into the soil. Rake an area until you have a fine tilth of crumbly earth. Then scratch out shallow lines (5mm deep). Scatter seeds thinly through the lines and lightly cover with soil. Kept moist, most seeds will germinate within one month or less.

Whatever you are sowing or collecting, growing from seed is a gratifying process. Not only does it generate new plants for free but it also allows you to engage in the complete cycle of life in your garden.

Collecting, sowing and growing your own seeds is one of the great joys of gardening.

Moving bulbs

It's highly likely that the garden you are reviving will have bulbs growing in it somewhere. Previous owners may have planted them or they will have arrived of their own accord via wildlife and the wind. Moving or splitting them is not a difficult task but the timing for this is imperative. The bulbs you are most likely to find in an established garden are grape hyacinths, daffodils, tulips, bluebells, snowdrops and alliums. All of these flower at different times and therefore need splitting and moving at different times, too. Some bulbs, such as grape hyacinths and snowdrops, have traditionally been moved 'in the green', shortly after flowering when they still have fresh leaves on them. They can be speedily lifted with a trowel and settled into their new location, which may be either another part of the garden or on the peripheries of the existing group as a means of widening it. Contemporary thinking also suggests these two plants can be left until mid-summer, when all the leaves have died off, before they are moved.

Daffodils are so rugged I dare say they could be moved at any time, but, to be sure, mark their positions with canes in spring, then wait until late summer to relocate. Tulips are a different matter. Many of them are short-lived and not worth moving but if you have any of the egg-shaped Darwin Hybrids, species, *Tulipa* 'Queen of Night' or old-fashioned red and yellow forms, they are worth a shot. Wait until after flowering and the leaves have begun to die down before moving them, encased in a clod of soil, to the new location.

Bluebells are as tough as old boots, so much so that I've even moved them in full flower and they barely seemed to notice. Ideally wait until after flowering when they have begun to die down. And don't forget to collect and scatter seed from their dried heads in the process.

All of the bulbs I've noted will appreciate a dressing of potash on the soil surface of the area they've been planted in to help bolster new roots.

Overgrown ponds

Ponds have the potential to get out of hand more quickly than most areas of the garden, thanks to the rampancy of aquatic plants. Left unchecked the likes of reeds, oxygenators, marginal plants and lilies can choke a pond to the point that it is no longer an obvious body of water. Bringing such water features back to life is a fun, if slightly stinky and slimy, task.

The time to tackle wayward watercourses is very early autumn. This ensures the minimum amount of wildlife is disrupted. Start by dragging out excessive mats of oxygenators and floating plants. Leave them and the other spoils of your clearance beside the pool for a day or so, so any trapped creatures can wriggle back into the pool. Next, tackle the marginal plants on the upper shelf of the pool. Each plant is likely to have a pond basket somewhere among it roots that would have been its original home before it burst out. Save these as they can be used for the replant. Most 'marginals' are tough plants, so setting to with a kitchen knife to reduce them to half or a quarter of their current root size will not cause them a problem. Reuse the aquatic baskets where you can, using aquatic compost to repot the runaways. With the surface and sub-surface plants tackled, it's time to set to on the deep-water plants such as lilies. These can take some hauling out. Once on dry land, choose and remove several of the actively growing rhizomes, cutting them back to 30cm and replanting them in baskets ready for reimmersion.

During the process of clearing your pond, you may discover that it is silted up or full of sludge. To rectify this, use a submersible pump, available from hire shops, to remove

Excessive nutrient levels in un-maintained ponds can trigger rampant algae and duckweed growth.

the water. Then silty sludge can be removed using buckets and added to the compost heap, along with all the excess plants. Once refilled the pool may look cloudy for a few days but will quickly settle and the newly potted plants will produce fresh roots before winter sets in.

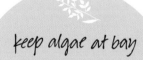

keep algae at bay

Grey or black organic dyes can be added to ponds to prevent algae growth, with no harm to fish or plants

layer in

The 'bones' of a revived garden, such as renovated shrubs, trees, borders and meadow areas, can provide a perfect canvas on which to 'layer' a new palette of plants. Layering not only allows the new bits of the garden to be embraced and intertwined with the old but also has a host of other benefits. It can extend the season of flowering interest in an area or on a specific plant. It can also add extra seasons of interest. For example, a planting that predominantly flowers in spring can have a range of summer and autumn species added to it to keep the area dynamic for an extended period. Layering can also enhance the colour and vibrancy of existing foliage and flowers by pairing them with colours that will make them 'sing'.

Plants to add to existing trees and shrubs

Only a select batch of climbing and scandent plants are suited to growing over, up or through existing trees and shrubs. They tend to have many shared characteristics such as fast growth, fine twining stems, light foliage and flowers that are produced on this season's stems.

Many of these plants will not grow well if you plant them as young specimens around the shady bases of existing shrubs and trees so, especially in the first season, size matters. Whether you are trying to establish scandent perennials, permanent climbers or annual climbers, get them to a decent size in a pot first. Aim for 1m+ of stems that can be lightly attached to the 'host' with twine until the new plant gets a grip and starts hauling itself through and over the host. These plants will thank you for the cool root zone provided by the shade of trees and shrubs so long as the top is in the sun from day one. Most garden-centre climbers tend to be on an 80cm–1m cane so this only really presents a challenge for annual climbers, which you'll need to nurture in a pot until they reach the all-important 1m.

Delicate twinning climbers such as tropaeolum and lathyrus are ideal for scrambling through existing plants.

Of the annual climbers, there a few on which I rely: *Cobaea scandens*, *Thunbergia alata* and *Ipomoea lobata*. All will reach at least 1.5m in one growing year and although their foliage is relatively fulsome it is not so dense as to compromise the host plant. Coboea is known as the cup and saucer vine as its flowers, with a bit of imagination, have that form. And it's worth knowing that despite it being grown as an annual it is actually a perennial, meaning if it's in a sheltered enough spot it will return each year. Thunbergia is not hardy enough to do that but it produces a mass of twining stems smothered in black-centred orange flowers. A real spectacle, it looks particularly smart when allowed to rampage over shrubs such as *Elaeagnus* 'Quicksilver' or green-and-gold variegated plants. *Ipomoea lobata* is a quirky

climber with rows of shrimp-like flowers graduating from cream, through yellow, orange and red. It reads well against virtually any foliage and flowers from June to October.

For more permanent 'layer' plants, several forms of rambling rose and clematis work well. Rampant ramblers such as white *Rosa* 'Wedding Day' or the bright red *R.* 'Rambling Rosie' are only suited to colonising large trees but add another layer of interest with ease. They often work best on evergreens such as pines or holly oaks. Of the clematis, the Group-3 forms work best for layering. This is because they are pruned to 20cm from the ground each spring, meaning host shrubs are not overburdened with a build-up of many

Pairing climbers

Climbing plants can often be grown through one another in a small space. Pair roses and clematis or annuals such as thunbergia and coboea together for fuller, longer displays.

Opposite page: Dicentra scandens on hypericum. 1: Tropaeolum through salvia. 2: Solanum on acacia. 3: Ipomea on cynara.

years of foliage and stems. Favourites of mine include the violet *Clematis* 'Polish Spirit', the pinky-red *C.* 'Princess Diana' and the dusky-purple double-flowered *C.* 'Purpurea Plena Elegans'. But the choice of both rambling roses and Group- 3 clematis is huge so there are sure to be colours and forms to suit your taste and the trees and shrubs you wish to dress up with another layer of interest.

Among other climbing plants that can be used in this way *Tropaeolum ciliatum* works well due to its thread-like foliage and delicate flowers, which almost become part of their host. This plant is more than at home threading through the stems of *Salvia confertiflora*. *Solanum jasminoides* 'Album' can also work well scrambling through small to medium trees. Grown in this

way it has a delicate ethereal quality when bobbling twixt the fragile blue foliage of *Acacia baileyana*.

Getting this 'layered' effect does not just rely on climbing plants, though. Some scandent species do the trick, too. This group of plants are real chancers. They are neither climbers nor ground-coverers, preferring to piggyback and lollop on whichever plant their seeds happens to germinate near. For this reason they do not achieve a great height but will happily cloak small and medium shrubs and perennials. Thanks to its lightness, *Dicentra scandens* can be allowed to colonise perennials where it works to extend the season of those that flower early in the year. Another scandent species worth a try is *Persicaria* 'Red Dragon'.

How to establish twining, trailing, tendrilled or scandent species

As I mentioned earlier, a scrappy seedling will struggle to emerge from the dark recesses at the base of other plants so size matters. Buy your 'layer' plants as large as you can afford: 1m is a basic stem length to aim for. Excavate as big a planting pit as you dare, without wiping out the roots of the host plant. Ideally the planting hole will be to the side or behind the plant. This position means that you'll easily be able to treat the 'layer' plant like an unruly comb-over and train it over the host. Add plenty of organic matter to the planting hole (see page 136) as the 'layer' plant will have to compete with its host for root space, nutrients and water. Keep it well watered for the first year of establishment.

Self-seeders and bulbs to add to mixed borders

Among my favourite plants are the ones we can't quite control. Not weeds and nasty pernicious thugs but the sort you introduce to one part of the garden only to discover that their will is stronger than yours and in no time at all they've decided to relocate to a different spot. These self-seeders and bulbs are what I like to think of as the wild or freer elements of a well-managed garden. Structure is all-important but to bring spirit to a plot some plants need to be afforded a little freedom to romp. And these plants will do just that. None of them are especially strong of root, so editing out any attempts at unruly landgrabs is not such a problem. And once these strong-willed plants have established a seedbank in your soil they will helpfully pop up wherever a scrap of soil appears, providing not only competition for the weeds but an element of continuity to your garden that will bring it together as a whole – rather like that last knob of butter added to a sauce to bring the flavours together as one.

Self-seeders can be broadly broken into four categories: annuals, biennials, perennials and bulbs. Annuals grow, flower and die in a single season, biennials do the same over two years and perennials usually take around two years to flower from seed, then continue to perform season after season for many years. Bulbs are usually a longer-term prospect. Their wild-sown seed can take from one to four years to flower for the first time, but the species I've noted here are at the faster end of the spectrum.

Easy self-seeders such as anthriscus, bluebells, allium and ranunculus are superb gap-fillers in mixed borders.

Verbena bonariensis and fennel freely self-seed.

ANNUALS

There is something awe-inspiring about the sheer urgency of annuals. Their unswerving determination to produce flowers and subsequent seed can see them go from germination to full-flowering plant in as little as six weeks. Of the most urgent are the likes of nigella and eschscholzia. Nigella, often known as love-in-a-mist, can produce flowers in around eight weeks. There are a range of forms of this easy annual, from pale to dark blue and a few whites. Sow them early enough and they'll set seed by early summer with a good chance their progeny will also bloom before the year is out. They are thin of stem and pretty wafty, so are best sown in a cluster or supported by other plants. Eschscholzia is nearly as quick off the mark, and like nigella it can produce more than one generation in a season. Often it and nigella will produce late-season seedlings that will overwinter and flower in mid-spring – a real treat. Eschscholzia hails from California, so it likes air and light around it. For this reason it's a definite border-front plant. The wild species orange flowers look extra vibrant paired with *Erysimum* 'Bowles's Mauve' but it is seriously bright so not one for the faint-hearted!

Impatiens are pretty speedy, too, reaching up to a metre in eight to ten weeks but they come with a warning. Several forms of this plant have escaped from gardens and are causing havoc to native species in Europe and further afield. Quite simply, do not buy, sow or share *Impatiens glandulifera*. However, pale-yellow-flowered *Impatiens cristata* are not quite so fixated on occupying every inch of the planet.

Other gentle self-seeders include *Nonea lutea*, a compact borage relative with pale yellow flowers in early spring, and the classic *Myosotis sylvatica*, better known as the forget-me-not. This pale-blue flowered annual will colonise part-shade areas and

Nigella and eschscholzia are reliable direct-sown annuals.

works really well around the low-light spaces at the base of large shrubs.

For real drama I adore *Papaver somniferum*, the opium poppy. There are many cultivars available as seed in tones of pink, red, white and near black. They flower at around 80cm tall with pale greeny-grey leaves, so are ideal grown through established herbaceous plants where they will freely hybridise, creating a new set of colours as the years progress. They are very reliable and their seed can sit dormant in the soil for years so they will pop up on cue if a space opens up.

On a smaller scale is the classic pot marigold, *Calendula officinalis*. Its iridescent orange flowers produce seed so freely that once it has a foothold it's possible to see two generations in a year, with some plants overwintering, ready to bloom early in spring.

Sow hardy annuals in shallow furrows in spring for an inexpensive summer display.

BIENNIALS

By the nature of their two-year lifecycle, biennials tend to be larger beasts than their annual counterparts. Year one is all about foliage and root production, readying themselves for a dramatic and often lofty floral display in year two.

Onopordum acanthium is a silver-white-leaved thistle reaching 2m with a penchant for dry soil and paving cracks; its dramatic branched form is countered by the pale foliage and mauve-pink flowers, which look fantastic with pastel-toned perennials. *Silybum marianum* is another thistle but about half the height of *Onopordum acanthium*. Its USP is its marbled green and white foliage, which is arguably more interesting than its pink flowers. Both of these plants do best in blazing sunshine.

For shade there are three easy biennials: *Smyrnium perfoliatum*, *Lunaria annua* and *Digitalis purpurea*. The smyrnium looks for all intents and purposes like a euphorbia, with eye-catching, lime-green floral structures. Year one sees it hug the ground with delicate foliage as it concentrates on making a taproot. In year two it heads skywards, reaching some 1–1.2m. Its self-seeding is so prolific that occasional edits are necessary but few shade plants are as obliging and vibrant. *Lunaria annua*, better known as honesty, is most recognisable in its seeding stage when it produces large, flat, oval, translucent seedpods. These can last through autumn and winter, slowly dispersing the seed of this tall white or purple-flowered border filler. For a pinky-mauve biennial self-seeder, nothing beats *Digitalis purpurea*, better known as the foxglove. It will colonise most areas from shade to full sun and, what's more, if you remove the flower heads before they go to seed there is a chance of a second flush of flowers. Do leave a few plants to go to seed though, to ensure it stays present in the garden.

Onopordum acanthium is among the most dramatic biennials producing a rosette of spiny silver leaves in year 1 and a 2m plant in year 2.

Digitalis (foxgloves) are easy biennials, producing a rosette of leaves in year 1 and flower spikes in year 2.

PERENNIALS

Self-seeding perennials are very different creatures compared to the annuals and biennials. Once they've colonised an area they are there to stay, so their ever-expanding population does require occasional culls to prevent them taking over. Fennel is one of my favourites. Its fine spidery foliage won't block the light to other plants and the delicate umbel seedheads appear to float aloft the sea of other plants. I've yet to find a perennial it doesn't complement.

Verbena bonariensis is equally light in foliage and flowers. I first chanced upon it twenty or more years ago in a Cleve West garden at the RHS Hampton Court Palace Flower Show. Then it was a novelty, now it is ubiquitous, but nonetheless useful. Although it is officially a perennial I've found that new seedlings from the current year often produce healthier and more floriferous plants. Of a similar lofty scale is *Verbascum chaixii* 'Album'. Its spires of purple-centred white flowers can last for several months and its self-seeding is not nearly as prolific as that of some of the verbascums.

On an altogether smaller scale are *Erigeron karvinskianus*, *Meconopsis cambrica* and *Alchemilla mollis*. All three are under 40cm tall. The erigeron is the most prolific in terms of self-seeding. It has skinny stems, fine foliage and a near endless succession of white daisy flowers which fade to pink. It will make itself at home in walls, paving and at the front of dryer borders. I've introduced it to every garden I've ever managed as its delicate charm is unquestionable and it's not so thuggish that it would present a risk to other plants. It loves the sun but will work in part shade, too, where *Meconopsis cambrica* also likes to reside. This plant hails from Wales. All other meconopsis are Asian so I suspect one day it will be reclassified as a true poppy. Its flowers are red, yellow or orange and they can appear for six months or more across spring, summer and autumn. This plant will colonise of its own accord but I also tend to snap off seedheads and shake them round the garden like some sort of crazed horticultural shaman calling for rain.

Fennel (above) and verbena bonariensis (right) are just a few of the easy self-seeding perennials.

BULBS

Getting a seedbank of self-sowers in your soil will take a few years, but to kick off the process there are two approaches worth trying. One is to sow seed in spring or summer, the other is introducing mature plants. Both have pros and cons.

For perennial, biennial (leaves first year, flowers second) and bulbs I usually opt for mature plants/bulbs. The simple reason being that if they are introduced as seedlings they will take at least one year to flower and set seed. In contrast, mature plants will flower the year you put them in, followed by setting seed which will flower in two years' time – so the process is worth repeating in the second year, too. The downside is that this approach is more expensive than purely sowing seed.

For annual plants it's much better to sow seed. These plants will grow, flower, set seed and die in a single season, dispersing seed for next year's plants in the process.

I rarely plant bulbs in groups, preferring to scatter them through borders to heighten the sense of rhythm and unity. Planting this way has the fortunate side-effect of placing sources of seed across a wide area, which ensures even greater natural distribution. Top of my list are alliums, not least because their lower foliage yellows in a less than dignified manner as they come into bloom, so emerging through other plants is the ideal way to disguise this. *Allium hollandicum* 'Purple Sensation' is the classic variety with large flowers that are unsurprisingly purple and sensational! The drumstick allium, *A. sphaerocephalon*, has a smaller head and is more egg-shaped with ruddy-purple tones. There are many alliums from which to choose, ranging from 20cm to well over a metre in height, with colours in purple, burgundy, mauve, pink and white. The spherical heads look beautiful left to dry in the border, so seed dispersal is a cinch.

My other suggested self-seeding bulbs (and corms) are much smaller and include *Crocus tommasinianus, Galanthus nivalis, Ipheion uniflorum, Cyclamen coum* and *Muscari armeniacum*. The *Crocus tommasinianus*, in my experience, is the most prolific self-seeder of all crocuses. It will spread its translucent lilac-mauve blooms through border fronts and even, charmingly, into the lawn. *Galanthus nivalis* is, of course, the ever-delightful snowdrop. It takes longer to spread than the crocus but is a welcome addition to herbaceous borders that hold little interest in winter and early spring. *Ipheion uniflorum* comes from South America, and it is not nearly as popular as it deserves to be. Its star-shaped flowers are white in the straight species with a few pale blue cultivars available. It prefers full sun but will survive dappled shade. Plant the bulbs among nepeta and other low border-front perennials and they will slowly expand their territory. *Cyclamen coum* is a corm rather than a bulb, but that makes little difference to ensuring it self-seeds. Grow it under deciduous shrubs in mixed borders where it can take advantage of the autumn and winter light to flower, set seed and form vibrant clusters of colour. The last and perhaps most prolifically self-seeding of all the bulbs I'm recommending is *Muscari armeniacum*.

It's best in full sun but I've seen it rampage away under hedges and light canopied shrubs. Grape-like clusters of intense blue flowers adorn it in spring. Beware purchasing sterile forms such as *Muscari comosum* 'Plumosum', as they will not produce seed.

Plants to add into long grass and meadows

Meadows or wild grassy patches can be among the easiest garden areas to maintain. Unless you are seeking to create a dreamy, perfectly balanced wildflower meadow, they are as simple to establish as allowing an area of lawn to run wild. Without specific 'meadow techniques' to curtail their dominance, the grasses will out-do most naturally occurring flowering plants, but there are several species which can be introduced and are capable of holding their own against the more aggressive of the wild grasses.

Bladed perennials such as hemerocallis (daylily), kniphofia (red-hot poker) and *Crocosmia × crocosmiiflora* work well here and bring hotter colours to the mix. Once established they can all be left to their own devices without the need for intervention. *Lysimachia punctata*, with its spires of intense yellow flowers can also be left to colonise a patch. For a slightly taller layer of perennials, try *Cirsium rivulare*, singalia and *Anthriscus sylvestris*. All hover around 1m tall and will self-seed or spread through the grass. Or for a more delicate look, the pale-blue-flowered *Geranium pratense* sits comfortably within long grass and, despite its apparent fragility, will thrive. Also suited to this environment are bulbs such as narcissus, camassia (in damp soil) and tall alliums.

Some bulbs and tough perennials will happily establish in meadow situations.

How to establish plants in long grass and meadows

For pot-grown perennials to gain a stronghold in wild grass and meadows they need to be introduced as mature plants at the right time of year. Planted in late spring they will have to do battle almost immediately with the fast-growing grasses and could be wiped out. It is much better to plant them in autumn, which allows them time to establish a sound root system. Many plants are engaged in underground chemical warfare with surrounding species competing for root space, so this method gives them the head start they need. Size matters, too: the bigger the better. Ideally I've always opted for 3-litre+ plants that are well rooted through in their pots. Add compost to the planting pit, keep the plants well watered in their first season and you'll quickly establish an alternative meadow.

Plants to enhance others with colour

Although reviving a garden often means removing lots of elements it's also about making the most of what remains. The foliage and flower colour of the plants you've chosen to retain can be cranked up another level with the addition of a new palette of plants. By cleverly pairing new foliage and flower colours with old, both take on a vibrancy and harmony that will give your garden a new lease of life.

There are many 'theories' attached to colour; how it is combined and the effect it has on other colours. To gain an understanding of how you can use colour to revive your existing plants it's worth looking at the colour wheel, which is a useful way of understanding the relationship between colours and how to pair or group them to create different effects.

The three flowers shown in the grid of nine photos opposite are profoundly affected by the colours placed next to them. Each new colour either brings out a different hue or lightens or darkens the colour it is paired with. The greatest vibrancy comes from pairing colours that are opposite one another on the wheel.

Plant colours can have a profound impact on one another, often changing our perception with their hue, tone or luminosity.

Paired colours from opposite sides of the colour wheel make each other appear more vibrant.

Analogous colours such as this 'hot' palette easily sit cheek by jowl.

You can see the dramatic effect that occurs when opposite (contrasting) colours are paired above. This visual phenomenon is known as simultaneous contrast. Pairing tones of blue and orange, purple and yellow or red and green makes both colours brighter. If you are seeking to create a more muted pairing, then put together foliage and flower colours that are harmonious and are lighter and darker shades of each other. The set of blues (pictured left) shows how easily this range sits together with no single hue dominating. It won't bring existing plant colours to the fore, but it will make them feel most comfortable with the harmonious tones that surround them. Another easy grouping is one where the colours sit alongside each other on the wheel. These are known as analogous colours, for example, red, orange and yellow as shown above right.

There is no need to follow all or any of these colour-grouping suggestions, but they are a useful place to start and will guarantee either harmony or contrast with your existing plants.

Here are a few further examples; if you have a plant with burgundy foliage try adding the colour lime in either flower or foliage form. The burgundy is, of course, a form of red, so it will shine against its colour wheel opposite of green (lime). Silver foliage can be dealt with in many ways; it is a neutral, so most colours sing out against it. Blues and violets look more intense and make it look paler, as does the addition of hot colours such as orange, yellow or red. Golden foliage can be zinged with the addition of purple/violet in the form of flowers or stems. The blooms of *Clematis* 'Étoile Violette', for example, look seriously intense against the golden foliage of *Philadelphus* 'Aureus'. Dark green foliage can feel sombre on its own but returning to the colour wheel you can see that by adding red in the form of foliage, flowers, berries or stems both colours become simultaneously more vibrant.

Lily of the valley pairs well with cyclamens.

refresh

Reviving a garden regularly leads to
fortuitous discoveries and opportunities.
The process of pruning, removing and
rejuvenating inevitably unearths a host of
microclimates and unique growing spaces.
To capitalise on these conditions, you'll
need quite specific sets of plants that have
either evolved or been bred to deal with
them. From adorning the undercanopy of
light shrubs to cloaking south-facing walls
with exotic blooms, there are plants to suit
every new environment you've discovered
or created. Introduce these species and
you'll not only be making the most of your
garden's existing framework but also
upgrading its seasonality, colour, texture and
form, leading to a total refresh!

Plants to grow under roses

Roses are the mainstays of many gardens but somehow lots of us have slipped into the idea that they should be grown in isolation or with groups of other roses. Perhaps this originates from the way European public parks are often planted but it need not be the case in our gardens. Roses have no shortage of wow factor when they are at full throttle, but even the best repeat-flowering forms rarely muster season-long flowering. For this reason I've often underplanted them with additional interest. I've generally chosen perennial species that can be mulched around when the roses are getting their spring dose, or annuals that can be sown in patches of scraped-away manure. All the plants I've used and recommend here are light in growth and relatively short in stature so they won't compete with the roses. Most of the floral tones are also delicate, meaning they'll sit alongside roses of most colours with ease.

Several annuals will work around the bases of roses but the three I recommend also self-seed, so in theory once they're established they'll just keep popping up year in, year out. *Nigella damascena*, better known as love-in-a-mist, is one, along with *Salvia horminum* and *Myosotis sylvatica*. The nigella has fine delicate foliage and blue cornflower-like flowers. Its seedheads are long-lasting and spectacular, forming ovoid structures shrouded with wiry crowns. In contrast the salvia has almost insignificant flowers but it's the bracts of this plant that shine. The top 10cm or so of every stem is wrapped in purple or pink bracts, which to the casual observer would pass as flowers. The real benefit of this easy-to-grow salvia is that it remains in colour for around seven months and rarely suffers from pests and diseases. The last of these three annuals is *Myosotis sylvatica*, or the forget-me-not. Once you've released it under roses it will freely self-seed and sustain itself. Its tiny blue flowers are a delight and almost appear to float among the delicate stems. Keep a close eye on it, though, and ensure good watering, as it can be a host to powdery mildew if it dries out.

Left to right Viola cornuta, Nepeta govaniana and Salvia horminum are delicate and resilient enough to adorn the base of roses.

Hardy, floriferous, groundcover geraniums make an ideal weed-supressing foil around robust roses.

Another easy self-seeder is *Crocus tommasinianus*. It's the earliest-flowering of the crocuses, appearing in late winter with pale mauve-pink naked flowers sitting just above soil level and providing a welcome respite from bare soil and leafless, thorny stems. By the time you are mulching in late spring it will have virtually gone back to ground, ready to emerge next winter. It vigorously self-seeds so it will spread across wide areas and even move into lawns.

Many of the shorter geraniums and aquilegia will also succeed around roses, along with the classic foamy chartreuse flowers of *Alchemilla mollis*. For a light see-through look, try the unusual *Nepeta govaniana*. At 90cm in height it's much taller than most of the plants I'm suggesting but the top half of it is open and wafty with stems decorated in a scattering of pale yellow-cream flowers. It works best with pale and mid-pink roses. For more of a groundcover effect, grow the white or blue forms of *Viola cornuta*. It makes dense mounds of foliage cloaked in large elegant flowers and enjoys the dappled light around roses.

Foliage is just as important as flowers when it comes to underplanting roses, and two silver-leaved perennials do a great job here. *Lychnis coronaria* and *Senecio cineraria* 'Silver Dust' have the palest of pale silver leaves, which bring light to the base of roses and set off any flower colour you care to think of. The senecio's flowers are fairly insignificant so it's all about the foliage, whereas the lychnis makes a rosette of silver leaves and then sends up skinny stems topped with magenta blooms.

Plants to grow under deciduous shrubs with light canopies

Lifting the canopies of tall, established shrubs is one of the key garden-revival jobs. Clearing out the low growth on mature woody plants not only reveals their trunks but also opens up vistas and, vitally, allows more light onto the ground. Bulbs are a useful first layer to introduce to this environment. narcissus, muscari, galanthus and eranthis will all thrive in this situation, slowly colonising the area and bringing spring colour with minimal effort. Allow them all to die down naturally, rather than removing fading leaves, and they will return every year. A more unusual bulb to consider is *Colchicum autumnale*. I usually recommend the longest-flowering plants but this is quite the reverse. It musters two weeks of flower at best. But the flowers appear at a key low point in autumn, their large pink blooms making striking contrasts with surrounding autumn hues. *Crocus speciosus* appears at around the same time and will naturalise in dappled shade as it has done beautifully at Sissinghurst Castle in Kent, England. It has pale blue-violet flowers with distinct venation and could not look prettier emerging from burnished autumn leaves.

For good groundcover under the dappled light of shrubs, heuchera, tiarella and their progeny × *Heucherella* work well. All form domed clumps of loosely palmate foliage that is essentially evergreen and throw up delicate wands of starry flowers in spring and summer. American breeders have become obsessed with creating an endless supply of new cultivars of these plants, resulting in leaf colours from brown and burgundy to peach, lime and red. Look out for those with an RHS Award of Garden Merit. This means they are

Erythronium 'Pagoda' makes for a spectacular spring display in dappled shade.

Above left Hostas and *above right Podophyllum versipelle* 'Spotty Dotty' provide dramatic foliage in dappled shade from spring until autumn.

tried and tested and won't burn out after the first year as some speedily introduced plants do.

American breeders also turn out an endless stream of hostas. These large-leaved perennials thrive around shrubs and there are over five hundred cultivars to choose from, ranging from heavy variegated foliage to upright plantain-looking leaves. Protect them from slugs and snails by treating with nematodes and spraying the foliage with a bitter-tasting deterrent such as Grazers G2. Both solutions are organic but will finish off the hosta's fiercest foes.

For quirkier foliage there are three plants I turn to: *Persicaria virginiana* var. *filiformis* 'Lance Corporal', *Podophyllum versipelle* 'Spotty Dotty' and *Dryopteris erythrosora*. All are unusual and quietly eye-catching. The persicaria is an abundant plant with lush attention-seeking foliage. Each leaf has a dark 'V' marking on it, which looks a little like the Batman symbol. So striking is this foliage that its pinky-red flowers pale into insignificance. Equally attention-seeking is *Podophyllum versipelle* 'Spotty Dotty'. It is far more sophisticated than its frivolous name would suggest, making a cluster of wide peltate leaves in mid-green that are smothered in large brown dots. It looks stunning paired

with the copper-coloured fronds of the fern *Dryopteris erythrosora*. Both reach around 40cm tall and will sociably grow side by side. *Hakonechloa macra* provides a fine-leaved contrast to these plants. It is a reliable grass for part-shade. I used it extensively for my 2016 garden at the RHS Chelsea Flower Show. Seven synabols got too much for the team so it became known as hack-mac. Use its mop-top form to bring lightness and movement to shady spots.

All these foliage plants create great texture, but what about some spring and summer flower, too? This can be introduced in the form of *Erythronium* 'Pagoda' and *Digitalis* 'Spice Island'. The erythronium emerges in spring with lush glossy leaves and small yellow pendulous flowers that have the look of a reflexed lily. It is not difficult to grow so long as you provide it with woodsy soil and reasonable moisture. It looks lovely with mysotis (forget-me-nots). Flowering later on in summer is the newly introduced *Digitalis* 'Spice Island'. Thanks to some clever crossing, it has a very different quality to run-of-the-mill foxgloves. Flowers are well spaced up the 50cm spike and have a 'pouty' lower lip, because one of its parents was what used to be called isoplexis. The colour is perhaps best described as peachy with a hint of pink. Elegance personified.

Top Digitalis 'Spice Island' and *bottom* tiarella bring floral interest to light shade areas.

Plants to grow against north-facing walls

The overbearing shade and dampness of a north-facing wall can make it a less-than-desirable spot, but with the addition of a few choice plants it can be brought to life. Shade-tolerant clematis and roses are a good place to start. Many red roses tend to perform well in shade or part-shade, holding their colour and flowers for longer than in sun. *Rosa* 'Danse De Feu' will do this on a north-facing wall, reaching some 3m tall and repeat-flower through the season. This non-stop flow of colour is especially important in shady spaces, and also delivered by *Rosa* 'Ghislaine de Féligonde'. I inherited this rose in a walled garden I once managed and assumed it was a 'climber' as it repeat-flowered but it is in fact an unusual rambler that flowers several times a season – a real rarity for this form of rose. Its blooms are a soft apricot fading to primrose and it is virtually thornless. It looks striking paired with *Clematis* 'Rogue Cardinal', whose

dusty burgundy flowers appear throughout summer. Together this power couple bring warmth to dank, dark spots. Another clematis I've used repeatedly on shady north-facing walls is *C*. 'Prince Charles'. Its pale lilac/blue flowers radiate light in the shade and being a Group 3 clematis its maintenance is no more complicated than cutting it to 20cm from the ground in early spring.

A more typical, but nonetheless desirable climber for shade is *Lonicera japonica* 'Mint Crisp'. It is all but evergreen, produces sheets of hanging foliage and is adorned with dark ivory flowers from summer until autumn. And did I mention it has beautiful marbled foliage and a sweet heady scent, too? It will enjoy the coolness of a north-facing wall because it hails from woodland, as does *Crinodendron hookerianum*, a Chilean plant that was brought to Europe in 1848 but has never really gained popularity. I can't image why. It's a graceful

evergreen shrub with skinny leaves and red lantern-shaped flowers the size of grapes. It will grow happily against the wall but plant it 40cm away from the foundation as it needs good moisture that won't be found in the rain shadow of a north-facing wall. For more subtle colour, try *Ribes laurifolium*. Its pale creamy-lime flowers appear in spring, bringing with them a freshness and light. Grow it free-form against the wall or train it in a fan shape. This also works for the red-flowered *Ribes speciosum* (right). All that said, the easiest possible win for a north-facing wall is *Trachelospermum jasminoides*. It may not be the most exotic or unusual plant but it delivers. Its twining stems will quickly haul themselves up any support provided and send out a long succession of highly scented, white jasmine-like flowers. Foliage is evergreen but does take on a few ruddy hints in autumn. It can reach 10m, but can be easily maintained at 3m.

Trachelospermum jasminoides, Rosa 'Ghislaine de Féligonde' and lonicera all bring long runs to colour and scent to shady walls.

Plants to grow against south-facing walls

A south-facing wall is a real gift in the garden. Thanks to the heat retention and protection it provides, a whole palette of plants that would otherwise be impossible to grow are within grasping distance. Species from the southern hemisphere and the Mediterranean regions will thrive in this most useful of microclimates. Some are 'wall shrubs' that can be planted and left to get on with it. Others are climbers and will require a structure of some description to climb or be tied into. Trellis is a quick fix but my preferred method is vine eyes and straining wire. Aim to install wires at 30cm intervals horizontally up the wall. It will work for most climbers and unlike trellis will not rot and collapse after a few years.

Mandevilla laxa is one of the most exotic-looking plants you can grow on a south-facing wall. It has white trumpet-shaped blooms with a swirl to the corolla that adds to its exoticism. The blooms are borne in clusters from mid-summer until autumn when it produces masses of elegant long seedpods that have the look of an over-enthusiastic French bean. They'll hold out most of the winter, too. This mandevilla is a twining climber so it will prefer a trellis or vertical wiring system. Expect it to grow 2–3m from the ground each year and provide a wall-covering of around 3 × 2m.

Exotic looking *Campsis radicans* is hardier than you might imagine.

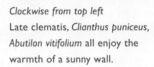
Clockwise from top left
Late clematis, *Clianthus puniceus,*
Abutilon vitifolium all enjoy the
warmth of a sunny wall.

Equally exotic is *Campsis radicans*. It is also a twining climber but much woodier and more demanding of space. Its long bell-shaped flowers are peachy-orange toned and produced for much of the summer. Keep it on a tight rein though to prevent it going feral and producing a swirling mass of flowers and foliage 5m overhead with nothing at the base. It is reasonably sociable so it can have a late-flowering clematis or similar growing up through it each year. For something truly extraordinary, which will get the neighbours' curtains twitching, grow *Clianthus puniceus*. It comes from New Zealand but looks like it might have arisen in the Amazon basin surrounded by toucans and hummingbirds, thanks to its large clusters of red bird-beak flowers. These are evenly scattered in clusters across the plant in early spring and occasionally repeat later in the year. It is not a true climber so will need its stems fanning out on the wall as it grows. The horizontal wire system is ideal for this.

Two further wall shrubs to consider are *Abutilon vitifolium* and *Myrtus communis* subsp. *tarentina*. Both will thrive in the warm haven of the wall. The abutilon has handsome grey foliage in the shape of a grape leaf and large, rounded mauve flowers. A single-storey wall is the perfect home for this plant as it reaches around 3m. If it's happy this can happen in as little as two years. The myrtus is not quite so speedy but does muster evergreen scented foliage and delicate white flowers notable for their hundreds of fine stamen. It can be managed at a similar height.

Combining these wall shrubs with climbers can create an easy tapestry on a south wall. Let the shrubs cover the base of the wall, where climbers are often without leaf, and the vines scramble around above (and in) them. Three easy climbers to do this with are *Passiflora caerulea*, *Solanum crispum* 'Glasnevin' and *Pelargonium*. Yes, really, *Pelargonium*. On a hot, south-facing wall many zonal pelargoniums can be tied in or allowed to grow through other plants and will easily make a 2m specimen. And it's not just in cities that they will do this, I've seen them do the same in rural Norfolk, England. If the plant is happy it can bloom virtually year-round. The flowering window of the *Passiflora caerulea* and *Solanum crispum* are a little shorter, at four to five months, but impressive nonetheless. The passiflora can be cut down to 1m in spring, ready to re-flank the wall with its exotic blooms and fruits or left to its own devices for a few years. The solanum, with its purple potato-like flowers, requires a little more restraint, unless you have 15 square metres of wall. Both are easy to grow and a quick route to an insta-exotic look while slower plants establish around them.

Plants for containers on a hot patio

Hot weather in spring and summer can virtually double the amount of watering required in the garden, so it's useful to have a set of plants that you can all-but ignore. Tough-it-out species from drier regions of the world can be container-grown on the patio and positively thrive on neglect, while lapping up the heat. These predominantly succulent plants store water in their leaves so can go weeks or sometimes months without water. Many of them will thrive outdoors year-round so long as they don't get excessively wet in winter. Hardy sedums and sempervivums will do this, happily hunkering down in their pots and soaking up the sun's rays with little need for water.

For something a little less run-of-the-mill, try echeverias. These rosette-forming succulents come from Mexico and have a near-verdigris tone to their foliage. Given their origins, these plants are very tolerant of blasting wind and sunshine but won't take a frost, so give them six months outdoors from May to October, returning them to a light but frost-free spot for the rest of the year.

Another Mexican succulent, albeit on a much grander scale, is *Agave americana* 'Variegata'. This beast of a plant has a dramatic silhouette and huge spine-tipped leaves. I always snip off the end of the spines by 3–4mm. It is not visually noticeable but prevents the plant from stabbing passers-by. I'm also supercautious when moving containers of this plant around. Tough as the leaves are they can get bent, split or marked quite easily and given that the plant may hold onto a single leaf for five or more years, it's worth being careful.

Two slightly more delicate succulent species, ideal for pots, are *Delosperma cooperi* and *Lampranthus brownii*. Both are essentially little groundcover plants from South Africa. They will grace patio pots with a summer of shimmering daisy-like flowers that open up

Top to bottom Lantana camara, *delosperma and lampranthus all adore the dry heat of a hot patio.*

in the sun. The lampranthus is the smaller of the two, eventually forming a 30 × 30cm clump, smothered in iridescent red-orange flowers. The delosperma will also reach 30cm but with a wider spread of 50cm or more. Its shocking pink blooms appear throughout summer. Both are borderline tender so will see out winter in warmer gardens but in cooler areas they'll need moving to a light, frost-free space such as a glasshouse or kitchen windowsill.

For a totally different look, consider the broad, silver grassy blades of astelia. This plant hails from New Zealand and is not normally cited as being drought tolerant, however, much to my shame, I've discovered it is! Years ago I managed to forget about a potted specimen of astelia for an entire summer. When I eventually remembered it late in the season it looked as happy as it had done in spring. Its shimmering leaves and tussock form make a welcome contrast to the foliage of the succulents.

It virtually goes without saying that zonal pelargoniums thrive in hot patio pots, too. Their abundance of blooms in white, red or pink add colour to what is otherwise predominantly a collection of leafy things. Two further plants to squeeze in are *Westringia fruticosa* and *Lantana camara*. The westringia is relatively new to European cultivation. It's an Australian coastal plant with fine silver leaves and it can be treated in much the same way as Buxus. It looks smart clipped into squat buns of 40 × 60cm and produces delicate white flowers nearly year-round. *Lantana camara* is not quite so formal. It makes wiry stems and an unstoppable display of flowers in orange-red and yellow tones that are irresistible to pollinators.

Keep all of these plants happy by growing them in a mix of 70 per cent John Innes No. 3 compost and 30 per cent perlite for drainage and only feed a few times a season with a half-strength mix.

Plants to grow at the base of hedges

The little strip of soil at the base of hedges presents a challenging growing environment. Depending on its orientation, the strip can be in full sun or full shade throughout the day, along with having a hulking great hedge leering over it and gobbling up nutrients and water. Plants that will grow in these situations are limited, but there are those that positively thrive on the struggle. Deciduous hedges present more opportunities than evergreen ones in that they can be underplanted with spring bulbs such as snowdrops, dwarf narcissus, grape hyacinths and bluebells, which will all arise, flower and fade before the hedge comes into full leaf. Evergreen hedges do not provide this window of opportunity so plants associated with them need to be up for a fight!

With good soil preparation and irrigation hostas will thrive at the base of shady hedges.

SHADE

The northern side of a hedge provides the greatest challenge, being shaded, dry and nutrient poor. The water issue can be addressed with a leaky pipe and the low nutrients resolved with mulching but there is no escaping the shade. Hostas can do surprisingly well here and provide a foil of contrasting foliage to a fine-clipped hedge. They also have the bonus of either white or mauve flowers appearing in summer. Once established many hostas are fairly happy in dryer soils so long as they have not reached Saharan levels of aridity!

The bulk of plants that can tolerate this environment are woodlanders, such as *Gillenia trifoliata*. This sophisticated-looking plant is not commonly grown but should be as it can flower from late spring to late summer. The blooms are white, delicate and star-shaped with a pink-brown base that sets them off a treat. Its leaves are crimped, slender and a paler green than many other woodland plants. Try it. It's a delight.

Also hailing from woodland is *Lilium martagon*. This is a small-flowered Turk's cap lily in pink with brown freckles. It is best planted through other woodlanders, such as *Tellima grandiflora*, as its flower appears on a single stem with little basal foliage.

Two plants especially suited to deciduous hedge bases are *Omphalodes cappadocica* and *Cyclamen hederifolium*. Both do most of their growing when the hedge is out of leaf and both bring low intense colour to this otherwise desolate environment. The omphalodes is a real shorty at only 25cm but punches above its weight when it comes to colour. Its blue flowers are produced from late winter into spring. It's also fairly unfussy when it comes to soil so is an ideal u nder-hedge plant. The cyclamen is equally a festival of colour but in autumn rather than

spring. It emerges from desolate-looking soil with a mass of candy-pink flowers that last a month or more and are closely followed by the stunning marbled foliage, which is nearly as lovely as the flowers.

SUN

The sunny side of a hedge presents some growing challenges but there is no shortage of species that want to grow in this low-water suntrap. One of my go-to plants for these situations is *Verbena rigida*. It will grow in dust, literally, thanks to modified water-holding tubers attached to its roots. Leaves and stems are coarse and wiry, forming clumps up to 30cm tall that are covered in a protracted succession of purple flowers. Once it's in you'll need to do little more than fell it to the ground once a year in spring. Of similar resistance is *Mirabilis jalapa*. This exotic plant from Peru also has water-storage tubers. One of the best stands I've seen of this plant emerges from under a yew hedge in Chelsea, London each summer to put on a display of red, pink and yellow flowers, which release their intoxicating scent at dusk.

Two further plants make the grade for me as tried-and-tested hedgers: *Eucomis bicolor* and *Liriope muscari*. The eucomis is a bulb that hails from South Africa, where it's more than adapted to low nutrients and intense heat. Its pineapple-like flowers appear in summer and are real showstoppers. The liriope is a more subtle creature. It looks like a grass but is a lily relative with tight spikes of purple flowers through summer and into autumn. It has a very rigid, hummocked growing habit so it works well in a formal row or can be mixed in with some of the other hedgers.

Top left Omphalodes cappadocica and bottom left Gillenia trifoliata bring colour to hedge bases.

Circle Mirabilis top right eucomis and bottom liriope add summer and autumn vibrancy to hedges.

Interesting evergreens for existing borders

The word evergreen can conjure up images of dark lifeless shrubs in inky graveyard tones, but lots of evergreen plants have a second strand of colour to them in the form of long-lasting and vibrant flowers. This selection of plants can be dropped into borders that are lacking an evergreen structure but have the bonus of bringing floral colour, too.

A real favourite of mine is *Rhaphiolepis indica* 'Springtime'. True, it does have a relatively dark leaf but from spring to mid-summer it is smothered in clusters of mid-pink blooms. It has a near ball form of 1.5m, which is not too dense and does not require pruning. Of a similar scale is the exciting *Mahonia eurybracteata* subsp. *ganpinensis* 'Soft Caress'. Now it is not too often that the words 'exciting' and 'mahonia' appear in the same sentence but this relatively new arrival does deserve that plaudit. It won Plant of the Year at RHS Chelsea Flower Show in 2013 and has gone from strength to strength ever since. What sets it apart from bog-standard mahonias is its light, delicate, nearly palm-like foliage. Overall it has striking texture, composed of layers of its skinny leaves, and will flower, unlike many mahonias, in autumn. It's the perfect plant to parachute into a revived border lacking evergreens and structure.

A more common evergreen, *Euphorbia characias* subsp. *wulfenii* is a real must-have, too. Its delicate grey-green year-round foliage is set off in spring by thick spires of flowers surrounded by limey-green bracts – about as fresh as an evergreen can get. It needs a bit of air movement around it but works well with perennials, so it can be slotted into a mixed border where it will form a loose ball of around 1 × 1m. Also of this scale and form is *Daphne odora* 'Aureomarginata'. I'm not a huge fan of variegated plants but the creamy-yellow trim to the sparse leaves of this shrub do not overwhelm. Like the *Rhaphiolepis*, it will never require a prune, but merrily puts out a month of ice-pink

flowers in spring. The blooms are so sweet that their scent can travel 10m or more.

On a larger scale are three reliable and bright 'evergreens': *Escallonia* 'Iveyi', *Pittosporum tenuifolium* 'Garnettii' and Ceanothus. Escallonias seem to have fallen from grace as garden shrubs but I can't see why as these 3 × 3m plants have so much to offer. It flowers from mid-summer to autumn with clusters of white blooms set off against its glossy green foliage, which in turn takes on bronze tones through the winter. It can be shaped, canopy-lifted or left loose and also makes for a useful floral hedge. What's not to love? Having said I'm not a fan of variegated plants, I'm about to recommend another one! *Pittosporum tenuifolium* 'Garnettii' is one of those inoffensive variegated plants whose leaf tones merge to give an overall effect of pale, dusty silvery-green rather than lots of shouty, contrasting leaves. Like the escallonia, it can be shaped and clipped or left to grow free-form up to 3.5m. Flowers are insignificant but through winter few other 'evergreens' feel so light and fresh in spite of gloomy skies and low light.

On the darker end of the 'evergreen' spectrum is the 4m high *Ceanothus* 'Puget Blue'. It's been a favourite of mine since I first saw it as a student 25 years ago. Sure, its winter foliage is dark, but it has a glossy sheen that lifts it, then come late spring the foliage all but disappears. It does not fall off but rather the shrub becomes so bejewelled with intense azure flowers that the leaves are no longer visible. It is short-lived but will bring at least ten years' joy to the garden.

Finally, for those brave enough, there is *Nerium oleander*. In theory it cannot take temperatures lower than 2°C but I've grown it in gardens that are regularly lower than -5°C. It is a risk, but a worthwhile one for light evergreen winter structure and flowers in pink, white, red or peach tones from early summer onwards.

Above Rhaphiolepis *below* nerium and *right* mahonia are all evergreen and florally bright.

Fast plants for screens and divisions

Reviving a garden is a great opportunity to rethink its layout. One of the classic design devices is spatial division, which can make an area feel larger by dividing it up. The divisions may take the form of fences, hedges or walls, but plants alone can do this job quickly. A selection of speedy species can create 'living walls' or divisions in as little as a single season.

The likes of *Atriplex atropurpurea*, *Datisca cannabina* and *Helianthus salicifolius* can go from a standing start to 2m+ tall in a couple of months. This makes them an economic way of creating different spaces and rooms in your garden. *Atriplex atropurpurea* is a 2m tall, columnar, burgundy-foliaged annual. It's really fast and self-sows, so once it's established in the first season it will continue to sustain itself in future years. *Datisca cannabina*, also known as false hemp, is just as fast but perennial. Its 2m tall arcing stems are covered in skinny pinnate leaves and topped with strings of tiny green flowers that waft in the wind. Its habit is more vase than column, so several need to be grown together to get a full screening effect. *Helianthus salicifolius* should be grown in a similar way. This delicate daisy sends up 2.5m stems that are bestowed with rings of fine pendulous foliage. It's deliciously light and floaty but its sheer scale means it works for division. It usually flowers by the end of a long summer but its small yellow daisies atop the wands pale into insignificance in comparison to the plant's willowy grace.

There are woody plants, too, that can achieve this mighty feat. Lavatera is the easiest of the lot, making a substantial stand of tall stems, grey-green leaves and pink mallow flowers in three to four months. To keep it fresh, dense and an effective screen, cut it back hard every one to two years to trigger fresh stems to emerge from the base. *Buddleja davidii* can be treated in a similar way and will reach at least 2m, possibly three, in a single year. There are many available cultivars in tones of blue, purple, violet and white.

The annual hack back that both the lavatera and *Buddleja davidii* thrive on can also be employed on two other woody screeners: *Eucalyptus globulus* and *Paulownia tomentosa*. Both of these catch-me-if-you-can trees can be coppiced (cut) to near ground level each spring. They both respond by sending up poker-straight stems to some 3m+. The eucalyptus has a typical silver-blue tone to its larger-than-average leaves and won't flower if it's coppiced annually. Nor will the paulownia, but that is more than countered by its rhubarb-sized leaves and exotic look.

For a straightforward, no-prune shrub that will create a screen in a hurry, little beats ceanothus. There are tens of cultivars in mainly blues but with pinky and white tones, too. Expect a 2m+ plant from a two-litre specimen in under two years. This great speed and value may lead you to ask, 'Why don't we use this as a permanent hedge?' The answer, sadly, is that it's very short-lived, often managing little more than ten years – live fast, die young!

Left Datisca, and *above left to right* atriplex, lavatera and paulownia can all make two-meter tall plants in a single season.

Border-front plants

So many plants fit into the category of 'border-fronter', needing little more than 'being short' to qualify. But as these plants are on permanent display, at the head of the chorus line, they need more qualities than just shortness to fit the bill. My selection focuses on plants that are not only short but also provide several seasons of interest or are long-flowering. And none of them need support, deadheading or tinkering with to keep them looking good, all season long.

Annuals such as the starry blue-flowered *Isotoma axillaris* or angelonia, with its spikes of mini open-mouthed foxglove flowers, work well here. Osteospermums can also be a real boon. The hardy forms persist well but tend to produce blooms in trickles rather than explosions. Go for the 'bedding' types sold in garden centres in spring and they'll perform summer long in a magnificent array of subtle colour tones, from burgundy suffused with pale blue to the peachiest peach. For a more unusual annual, try growing *Nemophila menziesii* from seed. It's known as baby blue eyes for a good reason. The delicate cupped flowers are a pale but intense blue with a white centre. It's a real attention grabber, especially if it is backed by darker foliage or grown with a contrasting colour, such as pale orange. This can be found in the form of *Verbena* 'Peaches 'n' Cream'. I've used this small sprawling or trailing plant many times to complement pale blue tones. It can be sourced from garden centres and nurseries in spring and is an ideal border-fronter, with or without *Nemophila menziesii*. Its flowers fade through several tones of pale orange or peach and continue until autumn.

For long-term border-front planting there are mini woody shrubs and perennials that fit the bill. *Helianthemum nummularium*, better known as rock rose, is a 30cm-high shrub with a succession of sulphur-yellow flowers from spring until autumn. It has spawned many cultivars in red, orange and

Top to bottom Angelonia, jovellana, nemophila and *right* coreopsis have long flowering-runs with minimal input.

yellow that will all do the same thing. Give it light and heat and it will perform. On a similar scale is *Tanacetum argenteum*. This silver-leaved subshrub has the prettiest ferny filigree foliage you'll find. It does have small yellow flowers but it is the leaves, which complement any strong colour you might care to place next to them, that earn it its place as a reliable border-fronter.

There are plenty of perennials that sit with ease at the border front but there are three that are just that little bit more special. They are *Fragaria* 'Pink Panda', *Coreopsis* 'Limerock Ruby' and *Jovellana violacea*. The fragaria is, in fact, a strawberry, but an ornamental one. It makes a succession of cheery-faced pink flowers that bobble around on top of typically pleated strawberry foliage from late spring to autumn. The coreposis has a more delicate look. Many forms of this plant tend to be a brash yellow but this cultivar has a dome of fine foliage topped with cosmos-like burgundy flowers. It won't reach much more than 30 × 30cm and looks beautiful against blue or silver foliage. A little taller, at 40cm, is the utterly divine *Jovellana violacea*. Its flowers look a little like a cross between slipper flowers, an orchid and PAC-MAN! They are pea-sized and mauve with an eggy-yellow throat speckled in orange-brown freckles. A true beauty from Chile, this plant will flower through summer. Do stick a label by it, though; from experience the world and his wife will want to know what it is.

Mid-border plants

Reviving a garden presents so many exciting opportunities, not least the possibility of extending existing planting areas. If space allows, try to make mixed and herbaceous borders at least 3m deep, ideally 5m. This size of bed allows for three to four substantial tiers of plants from front to back. Aim to allocate one-fifth of the bed's depth for border-fronters and two-fifths for border-backers, leaving you with the remaining two-fifths for mid-border plants. These midway species are likely to be the dominant focus in the bed and therefore ought to be as long-performing and captivating as possible.

I aim for either large-flowered species – those that repeat endlessly – or plants that have a couple of seasons of interest. *Salvia × jamensis* 'Raspberry Royale' fits the bill perfectly. It's 1m high, flowers from late spring to autumn and is easy to care for. It has a woody structure that can be cut back by half or more in spring to ensure a good show of its rich raspberry-toned flowers. Its small but numerous blooms can be balanced with larger-flowering species such as *Anthriscus sylvestris* 'Vicar's Mead' or *Zantedeschia aethiopica* 'Crowborough'. The anthriscus is similar to the wild parsley that adorns country lanes across Europe. The thing that sets it apart and earns it a place in ornamental gardens is its deep burgundy foliage and large, dusty-plum-coloured flowers. These are a washed-out shade of the salvia, meaning the two plants pair well together. The zantedeschia makes for a more dramatic contrast. Its flowers are large and embody the exotic with their single white petal wrapped around a bright yellow spadix. It does best on a moist soil but will adapt to most situations and can be split and divided every few years to stop it getting too bulky.

Verbascums are another perennial that can make a striking mid-border contrast, thanks

to their spires of flowers that last through much of summer. *Verbascum* 'Cotswold Beauty' produces spikes up to 1.2m tall that are smothered in peachy blooms, centred with purple stamens. Its subtle tones work especially well with *Amsonia tabernaemontana*. This blocky perennial has dark willowy foliage topped with clusters of pale blue starry flowers from spring to mid-summer. It reaches around 70cm, does not need staking and is very long-lived – a perfect mid-border performer.

Carrying on the colour from mid-summer onwards are *Hemerocallis*, better known as daylilies. They are available in every possible colour, bar blue, and are among the most reliable border plants. Their foliage is a dome of strappy leaves, giving rise to a succession of compact lily-like flowers. *Hemerocallis* 'Stafford' is a particular favourite of mine for its multi-toned red blooms with yellow midribs.

For something a little more unusual, try *Asclepias tuberosa*. Commonly known as milkweed, this American perennial reaches some 90cm before displaying its clusters of wonderfully complex orange flowers, which are irresistible to butterflies. I've successfully paired it in the past with one of the few big annuals that can be relied upon mid-border: *Cosmos bipinnatus* 'Purity'. The large clean white blooms of this cosmos appear from summer to autumn on top of and amongst its light, feathery foliage. For more long-flowering border plants, see my book *365 Days of Colour in Your Garden*.

Left Verbascum and *right top to bottom* amsonia, perouskia, asclepias and salvia bring colour and longevity to the mid-border

Border-back plants

There is something very special about plants that can go from diminutive spring shoots to 3m tall in a matter of months. These giants of the perennial world are prime candidates for the back of mixed or herbaceous borders. Lots of them tend to focus their efforts on height rather than width so have a relatively small footprint, which is a real bonus in smaller spaces. There are shrubs that take this tall and skinny form, too, making them ideal border-backers. One of the best is *Abutilon × suntense* 'Jermyns'. The lightness of its stems makes it seem more like a herbaceous plant, not to mention its succession of pale lilac-purple flowers, which appear throughout summer and autumn. It needs sun to thrive so don't introduce a 20cm specimen, as it will be instantly shaded out at the back; get it up to 1m or more before planting it. Staking also helps, as this plant can be a bit lollopy. Its colour tones look especially choice when paired with the pale yellow-green blooms of the lofty *Cephalaria gigantea*. This scabious relative reaches at least 2m each season and bulks up fast. Split it every few years to prevent it becoming monstrous. *Galega officinalis*, also known as goat's rue, is equally tall. It is a pea relative with typical pinnate leaves and clustered spikes of mauve flowers. It is a deft self-seeder, so once you have it you'll be able to share its progeny with friends. Like the cephalaria it should not need staking.

To get the most cohesive look from border-backers it's often worth repeating a few key species through the bed. Two plants I've done this with a few times are sanguisorba and thalictrum. Both have a see-through quality, which means repeating them won't block out other plants but rather create dynamic associations you might not have thought of. *Sanguisorba tenuifolia* 'Pink Elephant' is a striking cultivar reaching 1.5m tall and topped with bobbly flowers of a rich pink. Sanguisorbas are part of the European plant vocabulary, thanks to the legendary plantsman and designer Piet Oudolf, who regularly uses them in his New Wave planting schemes. *Thalictrum* 'Elin' has many similar attributes to the sanguisorba but reaches a lofty 2.5m. Its glaucous blue foliage is delicate and looks stunning topped with its pink-budded white flowers.

For a chunkier look to close off the back of the bed, choose tall perennials with dense foliage and plenty of bulk. *Helianthus* 'Lemon Queen' and *Aruncus dioicus* fit the bill here. Both can top 2m and both muster eight weeks or more of flowers. The aruncus has a vase habit with drooping plumes of fluffy white flowers arching out from the centre. It's so buxom that it feels more like a shrub. It does not require staking and can be divided in spring. The helianthus can be propagated in the same way. I've planted it in every garden I've ever owned or looked after, simply because it is robust, tall, reliable and generates a succession of pale yellow daisies from late summer through autumn.

Top Galega *bottom* sanguisorba *right* thalictrum provide tall columnar structure to border backs.

Choosing drought tolerant
resilient plants for hot spots
means you'll barely need to water.

Plants for suntraps

While reviving your garden you'll undoubtedly notice the hot spots. Parts of the plot that retain heat, such as south-facing courtyards, walls or enclosures, are special microclimates that ought to be cherished. They are the best bits of the garden in which to site a seating area but they are also perfect for a mix of South African and Mediterranean plants that just love to bake. Bearded irises are an obvious choice here, as they like to get cooked in a hot dry environment, but they only flower for a few weeks so there are better options with greater longevity. *Tulbaghia violaceia* is one such plant. It blooms from late spring to autumn with a series of long stems carrying a cluster of small pink flowers emerging from its grassy blades. Maintenance entails little more than removing spent stems and dead leaves once a year – ten minutes' input for six months' flowers has always seemed a very reasonable deal to me. Also bulbous but on a larger scale is *Amaryllis belladonna*. It comes into flower in autumn, just as everything else is collapsing, and grabs attention with its pale-pink lily-like flowers. They appear minus leaves so work best emerging from gravel or similar. Try them right at the base of a wall where they'll enjoy the rain shadow, free drainage and retained heat. They eventually make strappy leaves once the flowers have faded.

Dierama pulcherrimum and *Dietes bicolor* are two other bladed species that will thrive alongside *Amaryllis belladonna*. These two South Africans come from hot and quite dry environments so they can more than cope with European suntraps. *Dierama pulcherrimum* is often known as angel's fishing rod as its flower stems are tall, arching and adorned with rich-pink pendulous blooms. It can take its time to flower so buy the biggest plant possible and you'll have 'fishing rods' bejewelled with blooms in the first couple of years. Less dramatic but with a subtle charm of its own is *Dietes bicolor*. Not commonly grown in Europe, it will thrive in a suntrap thanks to its adaptations, including stiff sword-like leaves. Flowers are creamy with three brown blotches to the centre and for all intents and purposes it looks like a flattened iris, whose family, of course, it comes from.

All lavenders will love the dry heat of a suntrap but avoid the obvious forms and grow a more unusual wild species. *Lavandula pinnata* has all the scent and colour of run-of-the-mill lavenders but delicate silver ferny-looking leaves and flowers that have a more geometric quality. It's easy to propagate from semi-ripe cuttings pushed into sand, too.

For a contrast to the lightness of the other plants in this list, try *Melianthus major*. It is a tenderish shrubby plant with serrated blue-green leaves and, if you bake it enough, brick-red flowers. Allow space for it to spread 1.5 × 1.5m.

A hot spot would not feel right without some cactus-like spinyness. *Eryngium × oliverianum*, *Silybum marianum* and *Opuntia* deliver this in droves. The herbaceous eryngium is the best of its kind as its thistly flowers and surrounding bracts are fused with intense shiny blue. These flowers appear from summer to autumn and the heat intensifies their colour. Silybum (yeah, it's really called that) is another thistle but with a basal rosette of foliage in glossy green with striking white marbling. In truth this foliage is probably more exciting than the globose pink flowers it produces in its second year. Allow it to self-seed to bring continuity to the area. Lastly, there is opuntia. This cactus hails from Mexico but is very cold tolerant so long as it's on a free-draining soil. It won't fail to impress with its grey-green hand-sized pads (leaves) covered with terrifying orange spines. In theory it can reach 1m+ but where I have grown it in the UK it tends to splay close to the ground.

Left to right Eryngium, opuntia and dietes perform best in hot and relatively dry conditions.

Plants to grow under trees

Trees are more often than not the largest single entities in our gardens and worth upgrading and embellishing during the revival process. With thoughtful pruning, crown lifting, canopy thinning and soil improvement they can host a range of plants. Climbing species can quickly colonise their canopies with foliage and flowers, while bulbs, shrubs and perennials can flourish in their dappled shade.

Your trees are 'lilies' awaiting gilding and there is no shortage of plants ready to step into the breach. These sylvan species all originate in woodland environments, so are well adapted to the challenges and benefits they bring. Many woodland plants, such as bluebells, primroses and anemones, are in a rush, come early spring, to flower and set

seed before the leafy canopy closes in overhead. But getting a longer-term display calls for a different set of plants. These are the stalwart woodlanders that bloom in dappled shade from early summer to autumn. Perhaps the most reliable of the lot are hydrangeas. Their huge showy flower heads vary in shape from balls and cones to flat plates, with colours as rich and various as red, blue, pink, purple, lime and white. Starting in mid-summer the flowers transition through several attractive states before coming to full colour fruition. This blooming carries on until autumn when the flower heads dry and can be left as delicate skeletal reminders of the past summer. I favour the paniculata forms of hydrangea. Their flower heads feel more like giant lilacs than the blobbier mopheads. *Hydrangea*

paniculata 'Limelight' tops the list. Its flowers are lime green to begin, slowly becoming white and finally taking on pink tinges. Three flower colours across the space of three months from one plant can't be bad, right? It will eventually form a 2 × 2m shrub so it needs a sizable tree to sit under and shine. *Symphoricarpos × doorenbosii* 'Mother of Pearl' is another useful woodland plant for dappled sylvan shade. It's not as showy as the hydrangea during summer but in autumn its 2 × 2m frame is deluged with pinky-white berries that last into winter, a real respite from the shadows and lingering dampness of the season.

A small group of bulbs also thrive in dappled light beneath trees. The two I've planted time and again in various gardens are *Lilium*

Dramatic lillium lancifolium bring strong solour, form and texture to part-shaded areas.

Clockwise from top left Hydrangea paniculata, lunaria, hepatica and *hydrangea macrophylla* thrive in the dappled light beneath tree canopies.

lancifolium and *Cardiocrinum giganteum*. Both hail from Asia, have dramatic flowers and are surprisingly easy to grow. *Lilium lancifolium* has reflexed orange blooms speckled in brown aloft 1m stems. I've got it growing and flowering in 80 per cent shade but it is happier in a 50:50 light to shade setting. It looks best repeated across an area, whereas the *Cardiocrinum giganteum* is so dramatic it can go it alone. This Japanese woodlander puts up a 2.5m+ spike adorned with huge white lily flowers with a burgundy blush to their throats. It can take a few years to settle and flower but once it's away it's a showstopper. Flowering does not start until at least 1m up the stem so it can look handsome foiled with other plants, such as *Lunaria annua*. Commonly known as honesty, *Lunaria annua* grows as either an annual or abiennial. Once released into dappled shade it will slowly colonise areas with its gentle self-seeding. It's around 1m tall with purple flowers, though different-coloured selections are available.

The plant I regard as the most reliable woodlander has to be *Anemone hupehensis*. Just as the rest of the garden is starting to frazzle in late summer it pops into flower with all the freshness of spring. Its blooms are large and lofty, perching on top of impossibly delicate stems. There are many cultivars to choose from, growing 50cm to 1.5m tall and in flower colours from dusty pink to redder and white tones, so there is sure to be one to suit your garden.

If you really are short of ground space there are two squat herbaceous woodlanders to be recommended: *Hepatica nobilis* and *Stylophorum diphyllum*. The hepatica forms plants little taller than 10cm with a 20cm spread. Its flowers are intense blue, daisy-like and adorned with bobble-ended white stamens that give it real character. It blooms in spring, shortly followed by the 30cm-high *Stylophorum diphyllum* with its yellow poppy flowers that keep on emerging until autumn. Both plants are tolerant of most soils and together provide seven months of flower from a space little bigger than a shoebox!

how to wow!

Whatever the size of your garden, elements of 'wow' are important as they lead the eye and feet around the plot. They can be as broad and various as statues, arches, ponds, specimen plants and focal points. But beware over-egging the pudding. Too many stand-out elements can wind up in a visual battle that will overwhelm the garden and distract from its core purpose. There is no absolute formula but as a general rule avoid placing more than two elements that can be viewed from a single position. It's a cliché but true that less is more.

Specimen plants

The term 'specimen plant' has many definitions but I take it to mean species with a visually arresting silhouettes. Such plants are often symmetrical, sometimes quirky but always dramatic in their overall form. Palms and palm-shaped plants, such as tree ferns and cycads, feel especially striking, not only due to their unmistakable umbrella form but also because they are so different to the usual palette of loose balls, mounds and wafty perennial stems.

True palms are tougher than you might imagine, with several species well suited to growing in temperate gardens. Perhaps the best known is *Trachycarpus fortunei,* named after Robert Fortune, the great British plant hunter. It hails from cooler Asian regions and laughs in the face of cold winds and subzero temperatures. Rather than a typical umbrella form, this palm is more of a lollipop. It forms a cluster of palmate leaves aloft its clear trunk. It is typically left with its old leaf bases and horse-hair fibres shrouding the trunk but these can be removed and the ruddy stem polished to a gloss. Less common and not quite as hardy are *Chamaerops humilis* and *Phoenix canariensis.* Both will tolerate temperatures down to around -10°C. They originate from the Mediterranean and appreciate free-draining soil and oodles of sunshine. *Chamaerops humilis* is often multistemmed, making an explosive mound of spiky palmate leaves, whereas *Phoenix canariensis* has the classic palm form of a giant umbrella. To really get the neighbours talking, though, there is one palm that embodies the exotic and tolerates temperatures down to -6°C. It is *Washingtonia robusta* from Mexico. This daddy-of-all-palms has a stunning silhouette. Its trunk is conical and layered with the bases of old leaves in a compelling criss-cross pattern, while its crown forms a typical umbrella of huge finely-divided palmate leaves. This – just like any one

Dramatic tree ferns have an arresting fountain-like silhouette.

of the palms I've mentioned – is a guaranteed showstopper.

For a similar form, tree ferns always grab attention. They need winter protection, which is a bit of hassle but worth it for the perfect, unusually symmetrical parasol of fronds. They are sold by the foot and grow very slowly, so buy the trunk length you need from the outset and ensure it has a sustainability certificate.

Conifers are another set of plants with striking silhouettes. Generally I'm not a fan but a few stand out as prize specimen plants with bold outlines. *Picea glauca var. albertiana* 'Conica' forms a dense conical tree of blue-green needles. Its big brother, *Picea glauca var. densata* is a strong blue-grey with more upturned branches forming a near-perfect cone. For a more totem-pole-like look taxus and juniperus are worth a shot. *Taxus baccata* 'Standishii' forms a narrow bolt-upright evergreen pole,

never much wider than 40cm but up to 2m high. Or for stick-thin elegance, try the classic Tuscan cypress *(Cupressus sempervirens).* In theory it can reach 10m but that is highly unlikely to happen in a temperate garden.

Layered branches make for a striking silhouette and two plants do it especially well: *Cornus controversa* and *Viburnum plicatum* 'Mariesii'. They are both substantial shrubs with a spread of up to 3–4m but worth the space they take up. The viburnum makes stacked layers of branches that are adorned in spring with white hydrangea-like flowers – a real spectacle. The cornus is arguably even more dramatic, leading to its common name of wedding-cake tree. It can reach 6m high so needs a chunk of garden but a more compelling people-pleaser you will not find. It generally maintains a central trunk with rings of branches creating clear layers, like a wedding cake.

All the specimen plants I've recommended are more or less hardy, but a few tender species make for stunning container specimens if you have a cold conservatory, glasshouse or well-lit garage they can hunker down in over winter. Top of my list, and virtually unbeatable for sheer drama, is *Brugmansia suaveolens,* better known as angel's trumpet thanks to its vast bell-shaped, night-scented blooms. There are several cultivars available in pinks, peaches and white, all of which will make statement plants up to 3m-tall with a 2m-wide canopy. Other tender plants to consider include arid-loving *Agave americana,* with its broadsword-like silver-blue leaves and almost cartoonish silhouette, and restio from South Africa. These special plants look like a hybrid between bamboo, equisetum and an ornamental grass. Most have a striking vase or fountain form and coloured bands scatter up their leaves. Grow one in a large pot in acid soil to keep it happy.

Topiary

The idea of clipping plants into geometric forms dates back more than five hundred years. The Chinese and Japanese did it to an extent but it was due to the Renaissance gardeners of Italy and France that the idea became refined and embedded into global gardening culture. Topiary is often used on a very grand scale with knot gardens and symmetrical layouts but it can work in any size of garden so long as the topiary is appropriately proportioned.

I think of topiarised plants as being living sculptures that can be used singularly, in pairs or repeated through a garden. Virtually no shape or form is impossible to create. Over the years I've seen crocodiles, dragons, peacocks and even a couple in a moment of intimacy! Creating these whimsical pieces is a long-term undertaking, but for insta-wow there are pre-grown balls, cubes, spirals, cones, lollipops and columns available in a range of sizes. Most tend to be honed from *Buxus sempervirens* but *Ilex crenata* and *Taxus baccata* can also be worked into myriad forms. If you use a pre-grown specimen, work out the size you'll need before you purchase by placing any random objects you can lay your hands on in the spot you're planning to plant and bulk up the model of your topiary specimen until it feels about right.

In addition to the pre-grown topiary available, it's also relatively easy to turn a select bunch of existing garden shrubs into topiary sculptures. *Lonicera nitida*, *Pittosporum*, pyracantha, ligustrum and teuchrium will all take a trim and respond with the production of more dense foliage. However you choose to do it, topiary undoubtedly has the capacity to wow year-round.

Structures

From arbours and pergolas to treehouses and arches, garden structures are probably the most instant wow it is possible to create. Their sheer bulk and volume mean they will be visible from lots of views and vistas.

Arches are the fastest and easiest structure to install. They can be purchased pre-fabricated or you can craft them yourself. For such a simple device, arches have many benefits: they divide up spaces, making gardens feel bigger and add intrigue as to what lies beyond. They also create a vista that could focus the eye on another feature in the distance; and they can be flanked with scented, floriferous climbers.

The next step up in terms of scale is an arbour. These sheds-with-a-side-missing are charm personified. They work perfectly at the end of a vista or a long path and they draw people to them for shelter and rest. They can be purchased as flat packs and decorated to suit your space. I usually opt for a natural wood finish that slowly weathers, but they can be painted.

Another step up is the pergola. In the 1980s and 1990s they were ubiquitous in back gardens but seem to have fallen from grace of late. These simple structures, which are little more than a row of arches, can do many useful things in the garden. They divide up spaces, create rooms and entice people through their open-air corridor. They also work well as screens for unsightly areas and provide a host of planting opportunities, from roses and wisteria to grapes and kiwis.

For the ultimate wow factor, however, how about introducing a summerhouse, den or hut? They make for a charming discovery in the garden and I'd defy any visitor not to be attracted to one. Again, they can be purchased as flat packs at relatively low cost or built bespoke if you have money to burn. For advice on painting or adorning any of these structures, see page 204..

Simple timber arches, screens and buildings add structure and direction to gardens.

Water

Water has been inextricably linked to designed gardens for millennia. Its symbolism varies across cultures but in essence water is the bringer of life, light, movement, reflection and sound. Long before you discover a water feature, its burbling patter will have indicated its presence.

I have created numerous water features, ponds, waterfalls and rills over the years and they are often the primary focus or wow factor of the space they are installed in. As with any garden feature, scale is all-important. Not many plots can handle a full-blown 4m-high waterfall without it feeling a little

ostentatious, so it's worth thinking about scale before launching headlong into a project. Another important consideration is how the water feature fits into the landscape. I often encounter water features that feel as if they've landed from outer space and have no relationship to the garden. Consider the form of the rest of the plot before deciding on shape, scale and materials. Repeat these in the design of the pond, if possible, to ensure unity and rhythm. Location is important, too. If you plan to site the pool in full sun then you will need to flank the surface of the water with plenty of plants to avoid algae and weed building up. If you don't intend to plant, then be prepared

to use chemical treatments or filters to keep the water clear.

Courtyards or very small gardens often can't afford the ground space for a pond so wall-mounted features work better. A trickle of water running into a shallow saucer on the wall may not feel very wowing but it will bring movement, sound and light to a small space. Wall-mounted fountains come in both sleek modern designs and more traditional faux-Greek or -Roman styles with lion's heads espousing water.

On a slightly larger scale, covered water features can be slotted onto the edge of a

bed or patio. These work by having an underground tank covered in a steel mesh with cobbles or similar across the surface. Water then jets up through the cobbles and recycles back into the tank. To scale a feature of this nature up a bit, water can be pumped through an urn sat among the cobbles. They are not as dramatic as some water features but make a great burbling sound and are child-safe.

An even more impressive option is a raised or ground-level pond. I prefer a raised pool for ponds up to about ten square metres in size: the edge works well as a seat, people engage with it more and it's more evident as

a feature. Anything bigger becomes a major construction challenge so is perhaps best as a conventional pond. Consider the siting of both types of pond carefully. What will they reflect? Can wildlife get in and out? Can you sit near them?

The other significant decision when it comes to water features is what plants to grow in them. After all, the plants can make a major contribution to the wow. Water lilies are perfect if the water surface is still but they won't appreciate ripples and movement caused by exuberant fountains. Oxygenators, such as *Elodea crispa,* are important both to maintain water clarity and oxygen levels.

Many spectacular plants can be grown on sub-surface marginal shelves, too. One of the most dramatic is *Thalia dealbata*, known as the water canna. Its stems and leaves have the look of Roman spears bursting out of the water, while its flowers are clusters of purple blooms held on spindly stems above the leaves. For dramatic colour it is worth growing *Lobelia cardinalis* 'Queen Victoria'. This adaptable plant will grow both in soil and water. It has glossy burgundy leaves and bright red flowers. However, if it is big blooms you seek then try one of the Louisiana irises. *Iris louisiana* 'Extra Dazzle' is a white-rimmed purple form with large flowers through summer.

Views and vistas

Long vistas and dramatic views may feel like they're the preserve of large historic estates but it is possible to create them on the smallest of plots. A garden as short as 10m can have views and vistas created within it, it just takes a few visual tricks. A straight path, for example, may not feel like a dramatic vista but if you place an object at the end of the path, say a sculpture or urn, and then have the path get subtly narrower the closer it gets to the object, the path will appear longer. Another trick is to cut aligned holes through the fences, hedges and trellis that divide the plot. As the holes align a long vista or view is revealed. This idea is cranked up another notch if the end of the view provides something to look at. This idea is executed to perfection at East Ruston Old Vicarage in Norfolk, England. Strolling through the hedged walkways you suddenly encounter a moment where a series of circular holes cut through the hedges to reveal a lighthouse over a mile away.

True, we don't all have huge gardens and distant lighthouses, but with clever planting and landscaping it's possible to 'borrow' pieces of surrounding landscape and visually pull them into the garden. This technique has long been employed by Japanese gardeners, who are often working with compact plots, and it is referred to as shakkei, or 'borrowed landscape'. I have used the idea many times myself by installing planting in the form of trees or shrubs to frame or link bits of other surrounding gardens or landscapes. It's not rocket science, just a simple case of planting to block the bad views and leaving gaps to reveal the good bits. It worked especially well on a client's garden in West London. A lime tree at the back of the plot was ailing and needed removing. The client was worried it would compromise the garden's privacy but after scrambling around in the tree for a while I realised that removing the tree would reveal a series of other tree and shrub canopies disappearing some 300m into the distance. With the tree now gone the garden feels nearly doubled in size!

Creating views and vistas is possible in the smallest of gardens by means of screening and division or by 'borrowing' surrounding landscape.

Containers

Garden pots are more than simply plant-growing receptacles. Over generations they have become part of the language of our gardens and landscapes. Carefully placed they can become sculptural objects in their own right, sitting at the end of vistas or as focal points in plantings and hard landscapes. Repeated through a plot they bring rhythm and continuity. Planted they take on even greater visual impact as the plants are elevated and set off by the pot. They are also useful devices for growing and displaying tender plants that require moving to sheltered conditions over winter, or as containers for plants, such as acid-lovers, that would not grow in the garden's own soil. Used as single items they can be dramatic but if you cluster several together they really do become a feature in their own right. This is demonstrated brilliantly at the entrance to Great Dixter in East Sussex, England. Large clusters of pots are grouped together to show off the myriad plants contained within them. As the plants fade their pots are shipped away and new plants are added. It keeps the space fresh, vibrant and exciting and provides an opportunity to play with colour, form and texture associations.

However you choose to use pots in the garden, one thing is for certain: unity is paramount. A mix of pots in different materials and styles can feel messy and confusing. Better to stick to one material and then repeat, repeat, repeat. If you look hard enough, it's possible to find garden pots constructed from just about every material possible but the most common are terracotta, timber, steel, fibre, clay and plastic. All have pros and cons.

Container displays have the benefit of portability, along with the option of seasonal re-plants.

Terracotta is a wonderful material that over time takes on a subtle patina of salts, moss, lichen and algae. It quickly ingratiates itself to the garden but beware of frost. Inexpensive terracotta pots will crack and shatter in very cold weather so it's worth taking two precautions. First, buy the most expensive, frost-proof pots you can afford. Second, line the pots with bubble wrap. This means the wet soil contained within has space to expand when it freezes without cracking the container.

Timber pots are usually constructed from pine or oak. Left untreated they take on subtle silver tones or they can be painted, but either way they are relatively short-lived as the timber will eventually rot.

Steel containers often have a longer life, depending on their thickness, but can become easily damaged and dented. They too can be painted.

Fibre-clay pots are a relatively new idea. They can be finished to look like lead, timber or terracotta but will, of course, be a fraction of the weight. Look after them by slightly raising them from the ground as prolonged contact with the wet can fatigue their bottoms.

I don't think I've ever knowingly used a plastic pot to display plants but they can work OK in the short term, before the rigours of the sun puts paid to their structural integrity.

Lighting

Most of us rightly focus our attention on the garden during the daylight hours but with well-placed lighting the plot can really wow at night, too. Recent innovations have made the introduction of outdoor lights much easier as well as more sustainable. The new LED outdoor lights run at a fraction of the cost of conventional lights and can go for decades without replacement. Garden lighting is an art and science in its own right, but with a basic understanding of how to create different effects it's possible to design your own scheme. However you choose to do it, employ the services of a qualified electrician for the installation.

UPLIGHTING

Directional spotlights or wider-aperture floodlights can be used sparingly throughout the garden to uplight shapely trees and large shrubs. The light is usually part buried at ground level, pointing near vertically up the tree. The effect will see some of the tree thrown into silhouette with other parts highlighted with light. It is particularly effective on trees and shrubs with very pale undersides to their leaves as the light is gently bounced back to the ground.

BACKLIGHTING

This form of lighting can be used on a huge scale to throw large trees and shrubs into full silhouette, as if the sun is setting behind them. It is achieved with large floodlights pointing skywards or horizontally behind plantings, but never towards the viewer.

Uplighting trees and vertical elements in the garden bounces soft light back to the ground while highlighting their sculptural forms.

Backlighting trees and sculptural elements in the garden throws them into crisp, elegant shilhouette.

Spotlights are perfect for highlighting architectural plants along with denoting paths and maximising the gardens sense of space.

SPOTLIGHTING

Individual spotlights work well for highlighting objects such as statues, pots and features. The light units themselves are very small but have a dramatic effect. Reduce shadows on the object itself by spotlighting it from two directions.

FLOODLIGHTING

Lighting a garden in this way lacks the sophistication of individual spots and uplights. It tends to flatten the space and kill the intrigue. If you do require light across a wide area, try installing it at different levels on the side of the garden rather than the back wall of the house. This helps make it feel a little more subtle. Or why not experiment with

colours? I'm not talking about fairground-style illuminations here, just gentle tones of yellow, orange or even violet.

HIGH-LEVEL LIGHTING

Elevated lights, especially those mounted in trees, can cast beautiful shadows across the garden. As the light projects down through the canopy it is broken up by leaves and stems, leading to a dappled pattern being cast on the ground.

UNDERLIGHTING

This technique is usually the preserve of hard-landscape elements in the garden. The skinny LED strip lights now available are little more than 5mm thick and 15mm wide, meaning they can be attached to the underside of steps, pond edges, seats and raised beds without ever being seen. They help with safety as you move around the garden at night and have the benefit of throwing subtle light towards the ground, which in turn gently bounces back, providing a warm glow.

FEATURE LIGHTS

If the lights themselves are to be the feature rather than the things they are highlighting, consider using outdoor fairy lights strung through pergolas, trees and trellis. Or try them over a terrace area to create a gentle glow, or to frame a gate, arch or garden building. Recycled street lamps can have a certain charm, but keep the light level low to avoid flattening the garden with too much light. Stick lights can be effective for highlighting pathways but aim for downlight versions to prevent too much light flooding the garden.

Focal points

In essence a focal point is simply an object that draws the eye, but a well-placed one can draw the feet, too, and lead people around the garden. These points of focus are a real opportunity to wow. At their most basic, a focal point may be a simple urn or planter nestled into the garden in a spot where it reveals glimpses of itself from a few different angles. At their most complex (and expensive), they may be a statue, sculpture or elaborate water feature.

There are no hard and fast rules when it comes to choosing these objets d'art, it's down to your own taste. A sleek modern design might suit a contemporary sculpture whereas a lichen-covered stone statue could suit a more formal traditional garden. Before making any costly decisions, mock-up your desired focal point to scale and place it in situ … then add it to the Christmas list!

From inexpensive pots to pricey sculptures, focal points add direction, focus, allure and movement to the garden.

Colour

Painting objects in the garden is one of the fastest ways to craft a near-instant wow! However, without careful planning colours chosen and applied in haste can cheapen the feeling of the space and shout for so much attention that other more subtle elements of the garden get overlooked.

Choosing a colour for features depends on many factors. First there is the level of light. Gardens in northern Europe are bathed, for the bulk of the year, in a soft light that many argue is only suited to showing off paler, more subtle colours such as cream, pale pink and powder blue. Then there are the existing elements of hard landscape. How will your chosen tone work with the stone, brick and timber that make up the garden? And finally, how does the colour work against the backdrop of plants, which are, after all, the bulk of the garden?

The simplest way to try out colours is with sample tins, just as you would indoors. Paint some scrap timber pieces in the colours you are trialling and try them out on your plot. Is the colour so vibrant it overwhelms or does it pick out subtle elements of the plants and hard landscape? Does it get lost among the other elements? How does it feel at midday compared to dusk? Trial and error will give you a sense of what will work in your garden but there are a few basic guiding principles to follow in order to achieve different affects.

Even the smallest injections of colour can bring a space to life.

MAKE IT COTTAGEY

The idea of a cottage garden is in truth a fantasy borne of chocolate boxes and authors' fertile imaginations. That said, the feel of a cottage garden has formed in our collective conscience to such an extent that we have a set of rules: abundance, semi-wild plantings, endless roses and flowers for cutting. The colours attached to the fantasy have been honed by garden-show designers over the last hundred years and are actually a useful palette of tones that work in countries with low light levels through much of the year. To get a cottagey look, go for pastel-pale versions of virtually any colour. Think verdigris, powder blue, Suffolk pink, primrose yellow, orange so pale it's nearly buff and barely there, and pasty violets. All will work with ease and gently set off colours in their own palette, while making the hot and primary plant colours sing out.

MAKE IT DISAPPEAR

Some functional elements such as sheds and bin stores are necessary evils but have little aesthetic value. They can, of course, be planted to help disguise them but paint can help, too. To make a fence, shed or store 'disappear' in the garden, go for deep, dark, matt tones. A green so sultry that it is nearly black works brilliantly as it carries the same sort of tones as plant leaves in shadow and therefore objects painted in it recede into the landscape. Pure black can work, too, so long as it's matt, but it will show up white marks, dust and debris that get caught on it.

MAKE IT TROPICAL

Creating an exotic or tropical feel in a cool-climate garden relies on introducing some pretty vibrant colours. Many designers claim this is not appropriate for the northern European 'type of light' but, from experience, I think there is a range of colours that do work. They are not the shouty primaries but colours a few steps away, such as zesty lime, muted dusty orange, mid-violet, electric pink and so on.

MAKE IT MODERN

Much modern design is focused on paring things back and colour is no exception. To bring a sense of modernity to your plot go for pale neutral hues. Any tone of grey will work and makes for a useful backdrop for any plant colour. Taupe, buff and khaki are also easy wins. These colours don't scream wow themselves but they will show off bright- and primary-coloured plants in front of them a treat.

Make it Victorian

Renowned for their drab-toned interiors, the Victorians, ironically, opted for the most garish palettes once outdoors. Think formal bedding schemes with eye-wateringly bright reds, blues, yellows and oranges thrown together with scant regard for good taste. That said, transferring some of their interior colours outdoors can really work. For northern-European gardens, emerald green, burgundy, mustard, navy and inky indigo are subtle additions that will neither fight for attention nor completely disappear into the landscape. But do tread carefully, a huge shed in Coleman's mustard yellow might be a step too far!

restore structures

Early on in your garden's revival it's worth assessing the existing hard landscape, such as paths, fences and walls. These elements may end up being removed, reformed or recycled depending on whether your revival embraces a total re-design or not. The first question to ask yourself is whether these paths, steps, buildings etc. are in the right place for your needs. If not, then the process described on page 12 will help you with a re-design. If you are happy with the placement of the hard landscape then follow the guide for how to rejuvenate them.

Revive paving

The combination of weather and wear can degrade paving surfaces, but they can be revived with relative ease.

EXCESSIVE ALGAE GROWTH

The natural propensity of brick, concrete and stone to hold water on their surfaces makes them perfect breeding grounds for slimy green algae, which leads to paving becoming dangerously slippery. This problem can be addressed in two ways. A hired pressure washer will remove all the algae but does make a bit of mess in the process and runs the risks of loosening the pointing between bits of paving. The alternative is to use a garden disinfectant, such as Jeyes Fluid. Applied to the paving surface with a watering can, it kills off algae in around 24 hours so long as there is no rain. It does not affect surrounding plants but it will smell hospital-like for a few days after treatment. Expect to do this annually to keep paving, especially in that shade, clear of algae.

POOLING WATER

Gathering water is a sure sign that the hard landscape has not been laid with enough of a fall for water to run off or it's just not been laid flat. Using a hired angle grinder (and associated personal protective equipment), cut out the individual slabs and use a hammer and bolster to clean them up. Relay them on a five-spot mortar bed, 1mm or so higher than the surrounding paving.

Pointing broken out of slabs

Due to water ingress and frost, aged paving often loses the mortar pointing between slabs, bricks or stones. To revive the paving, remove the rest of the pointing using a hammer and bolster. Repoint the slabs using a 6:1 mortar mix (batched – see page 213) and a small pointing trowel. Finish the joints using either an old piece of hose to create a rounded recessed joint or the pointing trowel to form a ridge.

WEEDS BETWEEN SLABS

This annoying problem can be resolved in a number of ways. Hand-removal works but is time consuming. Alternatively, buy or hire a weed burner, which runs on gas and turns leaves to ashes in a flash. Herbicides can also be used here. Translocated types work best to kill off the root and avoid re-emergence. A more organic solution is to use a block paving wire brush.

INDIVIDUAL BROKEN SLABS

If you have discovered 'spares' of the paving material during the revival process then hold on to them as they may be useful replacements for broken bits. Trying to match like-for-like with new replacements is more often than not folly and the replaced brick or slab will forever shine out, announcing its newness. Unless a broken stone or slab is central to a path or key route, consider doing away with it altogether and putting a 'pocket planting' in its place.

LOOSE SLABS

Wobbly paving slabs are annoying, dangerous and likely to break in the end. Either do (as left) and 'pocket-plant' the area or reset the slab. To reset a slab, first lift it and clean off any mortar on the back. Next, using a 5:1 sand to cement ratio, resettle the slab on five spots of mortar – one on each corner and one in the middle.

Revive gravel

Garden paths, seating areas and plantings can look great with fine grades of gravel providing their surface. They do present a number of problems, though, as gravel tends to migrate, become thin in high-wear areas and provide a seedbed for weeds. Addressing these issues is vital early on to prevent future problems.

A MIX OF GRAVEL TYPES

A gravel path or planting area quickly loses its charm if, over the years, different aggregates have been thrown down. A mix of sea-sourced 20mm gravel mixed with pea shingle mixed with green granite chips is not a thing of beauty. The solution is time-consuming but worth it. Use a mix of compost sieves, chicken wire or wire mesh sheets to sieve through the gravel and separate out the sizes and types you don't want.

THIN PATCHES

Skimpy patches of gravel usually tend to be surrounded by thick patches where the stones have been kicked or pushed to the side. Solving this is simply a case of redistributing the gravel with a rake. If areas are really thin with no excess to the side then companies such as CED in the UK can match and supply your existing gravel as a top-up.

Excessive weeds

Ambient dust, grit and soil will slowly settle into gravel over time, providing a near-perfect seedbed for weeds. Those that are present can be removed by hand, or weedkiller can be applied, but to avoid this labour in future there are a few simple remedies. I'm not a fan, but there are several residual granular herbicides that can be sprinkled on to prevent future weeds germinating. I'd rather be diligent with a hoe every few weeks to chop of any emerging weeds before they get a foothold. Another solution, if the gravel is currently laid direct on soil, is to remove the gravel, excavate about 100mm, line the excavation with a geotextile and backfill with a Type-1 granular sub-base. The sub-base can then be solidified with a hired plate vibrator and the gravel returned. This will radically reduce future weed emergence.

Gravel can make for an attractive surface but requires regular care to avoid it migrating and becoming weedy.

Revive fences

The boundary to our gardens is more often than not a fence. They are highly effective and quick to install but are under constant pressure from the environment. Rain, snow and general damp will slowly degrade and rot them, not to mention the constant buffering they receive from the wind. They can often be patched up, but there comes a point where total replacement is necessary.

Softwood fences, even if regularly treated, have a limited life-span meaning they need replacing every 20 years or so.

WOBBLY OR COLLAPSED FENCE PANELS

These are simple enough to replace with matching panels from a local garden centre or timber merchant. Stop the new panel standing out like a sore thumb by painting it and the rest of the fence at the same time with a dark stain or paint.

ROTTING SLATS

As above, rotting slats can be replaced with standard timbers from a timber merchant or you can have timbers cut to shape and size for you.

ROTTING POSTS

If timber fence posts are rotting it's likely the panels are not far behind, so it's time to bite the bullet and replace the whole fence. I've investigated this a few times and it appears, in most instances, that it is as cheap to get a fencing specialist in as it is to try and buy the materials yourself – so I've always saved myself the labour and left it to the experts.

Revive decks

Thanks to a spate of makeover TV shows in the 1990s, gardens are now more decked than ever before. These wooden terraces are among the warmest and gentlest of garden features but left for more than a year without maintenance they can become lethal!

Unmaintained decks quickly become slippery as a result of algae growth.

EXCESSIVE MOSS AND ALGAE GROWTH

Decks can become like ice rinks if they are not well maintained. Some people choose to cover them in chicken wire to avoid them becoming slippery but to me that compromises the aesthetic far too much. The simple solution is annual maintenance. A pressure washer on a low setting works well on good timber to eradicate moss and algae. This can be used in addition to a garden disinfectant, which will also kill off the green slime.

ROTTING TIMBERS

Once the rot has set in on a deck it is pretty much 'game over'. Falling through a deck is potentially dangerous, as I've personally discovered! So the solution is to replace the deck using quality pressure-treated soft wood. Or, if you can afford it, hard wood, which, with good maintenance, will last a lifetime.

POPPED-UP BOARDS

Deck screws sometimes fatigue and rust, causing boards to pop up. These present dangerous trip hazards but can be resecured with specialist deck screws, available from builders' merchants.

REVIVE STEPS

An unstable or broken step ought to be your first priority when reviving hard landscape as it is potentially dangerous. Stone or slab steps are easily relaid, just like loose paving slabs (see page 209). Bricks are more of challenge and may require professional assistance.

If damage has occurred to the front edge of stone, slab or brick steps, consider turning the whole step around so the damage is at the back of the step where your feet will never venture.

If steps suffer from moss and algae growth, address this problem as per paving (see page 208).

Revive walls

A wall in a garden is a real blessing. It provides shelter, shade or suntrap depending on its orientation. These structures are often among the longest-lived in established gardens but can slowly and imperceptibly degrade, ultimately becoming dangerous. If you have even the slightest doubt about the stability of your walls then it is worth calling in a specialist to advise on work but for other matters try the following solutions.

LOOSE BRICKS

A poor batch of mortar in a wall or an area constantly battered by rain can begin to degrade and lose its pointing. Once this has been set in motion it is worsened by frost as water penetrates the wall and then expands as it freezes, causing bricks and mortars to shatter. Rectify the issue by scraping out all the loose mortar and carefully re-pointing using a 6:1 soft sand to cement ratio.

DAMAGED POINTING

The mortar holding walls together inevitably degrades but can be addressed using the method above. If the damage is extensive it is often more cost effective to get a builder in to do the work quickly and efficiently.

WEED INGRESS

Gaps in the mortar on the sides and tops of walls slowly fill with ambient grit and soil, eventually becoming the perfect germination spot for seedlings such as grass species and buddleja. As these wall-seeded plants grow, inevitably their roots expand, causing further damage to the wall. Pulling them out by hand can often damage the wall further so I opt for weed-wiping using a translocated herbicide.

Crumbling walls can be charming in a garden, but be sure to check on their safety and stability.

Seasonal Revival Tasks

	SPRING			SUMMER	
	Early	Mid	Late	Early	Mid
Planting containerised species	✓	✓	✓	✓	✓
Planting bare-root species	✓	✓			
Sowing annual seeds	✓	✓	✓	✓	
Sowing perennial seeds	✓	✓	✓		
Sowing biennial seeds				✓	✓
Moving shrubby plants	✓				
Moving herbaceous plants	✓	✓	✓		
Moving bulbs				✓	✓
Splitting perennials	✓	✓	✓		
Collecting seeds				✓	✓
Taking hardwood cuttings					
Pruning trees	✓	✓	✓	✓	✓
Pruning apples					
Pruning cherries				✓	✓
Pruning evergreens					
Pruning hedges					✓
Crown reduction prune	✓	✓	✓	✓	✓
Crown thin prune	✓	✓	✓	✓	✓
Crown lift prune	✓	✓	✓	✓	✓
Rejuvenative prune	✓	✓	✓	✓	✓
Prune HT roses	✓	✓			
Prune spring-flowering shrubs				✓	
Weeding	✓	✓	✓	✓	✓
Reviving ponds					
Reviving hard landscapes	✓	✓	✓	✓	✓
Create new layout	✓	✓	✓	✓	✓
Feed, weed and moss kill lawns	✓	✓	✓		
Sow lawn	✓	✓	✓	✓	✓
Lay turf	✓	✓	✓	✓	✓
Testing soil	✓	✓	✓	✓	✓
Improve soils	✓	✓	✓	✓	✓
Feeding beds and borders	✓	✓	✓	✓	✓
Double digging	✓	✓	✓	✓	✓
Mulching	✓	✓	✓	✓	

| | AUTUMN | | | WINTER | | |
Late	Early	Mid	Late	Early	Mid	Late
✓	✓	✓	✓	✓	✓	✓
			✓	✓	✓	✓
						✓
✓	✓					
			✓	✓	✓	✓
		✓	✓	✓	✓	✓
✓						
✓	✓	✓	✓			
				✓	✓	✓
✓	✓	✓	✓	✓	✓	✓
			✓	✓	✓	✓
✓	✓					
					✓	
✓	✓	✓	✓			
✓	✓					
✓	✓					
✓	✓					
						✓
✓	✓	✓	✓	✓	✓	✓
	✓	✓				
✓	✓	✓	✓	✓	✓	✓
✓	✓	✓	✓	✓	✓	✓
	✓	✓				
✓	✓					
✓	✓	✓	✓	✓	✓	✓
✓	✓	✓	✓	✓	✓	✓
✓	✓	✓	✓			
✓	✓	✓	✓	✓	✓	✓
✓	✓	✓	✓	✓	✓	✓

Index

Picture Credits

Photographs by Jonathan Buckley other than those stated below.

All images preceded with an asterix have been supplied by GAP photos
- www.gapphotos.com.

b = bottom   t = top   l = left   r = right   m = middle   c = circle

23: l: *Maxine Adcock
24: m: Peter Cassidy
25: tr: Peter Cassidy
36: bl: *Visions
39: tr: *Howard Rice
47: l: *Pernilla Bergdahl
49: br: *Howard Rice
53: bl: *Heather Edwards
54: bl: *Jason Smalley
55: bm: *Richard Loader
58/59: *Howard Rice
71: *Pernilla Bergdahl
78: tm: *Howard Rice
106/107: *Nicola Stocken
109: *John Glover
110: *J S Sira
111: *Howard Rice
112: *Christa Brand
113: tr: *Marcus Harpur
    bl: *Elke Borkowski
114: *Heather Edwards
115: *Marcus Harpur
119: t: *Jonathan Need
130/131: *Robert Mabic
141: *Carole Drake
159: br: *Pernilla Bergdahl
160/161: *Carole Drake
166: m: *Howard Rice
167: *Howard Rice

168: *Oliver Mathews
169: b: *John Glover
171: m: *Nicola Stocken
    b: *Geoff du Feu
173: tc: *Martin Hughes-Jones
    br: *Richard Bloom
174: t: *Martin Hughes-Jones
    b: *Howard Rice
175: *Marcus Harpur
178: t: *Dave Beva
    b: *Tommy Tonsberg
179: *Elke Borkowski
181: t: *Christa Brand
    b: *Martin Hughes-Jones
182: b: *Rob Whitworth
183: *Dianna Jazwinski
184: *GAP Photos
185: m: *Pernilla Bergdahl
    r: *Jarry Harpur
186: *Howard Rice
188/189: *Richard Bloom
200: t: *Elke Borkowski
    b: *Nicola Stocken
201: *Clive Nichols
204: *Steven Wooster
205: t: *Christa Brand
    b: *Fiona McLeod
206/207: *J S Sira

Acknowledgements

Huge thanks to...

Alan Gray and Graham Robson for letting us loose on their splendid garden, East Ruston Old Vicarage, Norfolk, for photography. Mark Holman – The Palace Gardener – for photography and access to his London gardens. Stefan and Gosia Turnbull, providers of a garden for photography. Suha Aranki, provider of a garden for photography and my wonderful 'surrogate mum'. Sue Richardson, provider of a garden for photography, along with friendship and rock-solid advice. Sharon Perez, provider of a garden for photography and for being the best and most supportive PA and friend in the business. Mary Ellen Taylor, provider of a garden for photography and a wonderful friend, confidant and sounding board. Will Tubby, provider of a garden for photography; a friend and true talent. My mum, for ongoing support and diligent proofreading. Dad and Rose, for use of the writing room and oodles of moral support. Jonathan Buckley, for world-class photography and many laughs. Tom Brown and Lady Emma Barnard for access to the wonderful Parham House Gardens. Judith Hannam, my editor, for keeping it all on track. Jenny Semple, for carefully crafted design and layout of the book. Alyson Hamilton, for delightful illustrations and friendship. The Growing Friends at CPG, Charlotte, Sally, Mary-Ellen, Penny and Alison – an inspiration.

For Believing in me: Rosemary Alexander, Chris Brickell, Christopher Bailes, Lady Amabel Lindsay, Kemal Mehdi, Ivan Tatum, Dick Scott, Doug McMurtry, Paolo Proto, Sharon Fisher, Lucy Hall, Kevin Smith, Clare Foggett, Simon Caney and Kyle Cathie.

For support: Katy Willimer, Rose Lowe, Valanna Quaile, Olivia Bailey, Clementina Immerzi, Veronika Rasickaite, Herve Moquet, Lloyd Bailey, Pia Ostlund, Dan Hedley, Mary-Ellen Taylor, Alex Walpole, Nell Jones, Andrew Mills and Sharon Perez.